A SPECTACLE

His friend was lying
steeping his pale fac
The slumberer's eyes were closed. His ....
heaved with the flow of life. His lips were parted in
an unconscious smile, and the lines of care and
work were smoothed, as if by magic, out of his wan
young face. Crouched on the man's body, his eyes
bright with an un natural brilliancy, was the live
corpse, Long. His white hands were buried up to
their wrists in the pillows. He had nothing but his
shirt to cover his nakedness, and his long
attenuated legs made him fearfully like a hogs white
spider. His throat swelled and collapsed, as he
steadily sucked at a spot under the sleeper's ear. A
low purring sound mingled with the lapping of his
victim's blood. His fiendish eyes glared into the
other's white face. His baggy stomach wagged from
aide to side in ecstasy. His sleek white back and
breast shone in the moonlight, and his red hair
bristled up with angry erectness. As he sucked the
other grew whiter and weaker. Lovely visions
seemed to take the place of his life's blood. As the
monster drank in the precious fluid, the smile that
hovered about his lips grew softer and sweeter. It
was just the opposite with the murderer. The
draught of blood seemed to intoxicate him. He
swelled with it. It flashed red and fiery out of his
eyes. It crimsoned his ghastly face. It thickens his
thin fingers and made his arms round and easy.
The monster grew less hideous and more devilish
with every drop.

BELIEVE IN VAMPIRES.

Rhode Islanders Who Are Sure That They Do Exist.

Instances Told of Where the Living Have Been Attacked and Preyed Upon by These Representatives of an Unseen World.

A MEMBER OF THE ANTI-VAMPIRE PARTY.

COWBOYS & VAMPIRES

THE UNDEAD IN NORTH AMERICA

John LeMay

Bicep Books
Roswell, NM

First Edition

LeMay, John.
    Cowboys & Vampires: The Undead in North America
        1. History—Pioneer Era. 2. Supernatural
        3. Folklore, Early Twentieth Century.

FOR DR. JOHN AND
THE SCARYCAST CREW

PREFACE

As I was preparing my last book, *Cowboys & Monsters: Vampires, Mummies, and Werewolves of the Wild West*, I was shocked by the sheer dearth of stories to choose from. At best, I thought I might barely scrape by when it came to that tome. However, before I knew it, the book was ballooning to be over 500 pages long! It was also getting a bit off balance with more werewolf stories than mummies or vampires. As such, I decided to limit that book to the stories that had more of an Old West flare. I also realized that there was enough material for separate volumes dedicated to vampires, werewolves, and mummies of the Americas on their own.

As such, I'd say a little over a third of the stories in this book you may have seen before in *Cowboys & Monsters*. All of those chapters are the same except for one, "Vampire on the Range," since I found some additional information on Nebraska's alleged 1895 vampire attacks. As for the stories I purposely held back from *Cowboys & Monsters,* they consisted of well-known tales like the Exeter Vampire affair of 1892, which took place far enough back East that I felt it didn't fit the confines of Wild West. The new material in this book isn't entirely comprised of chapters I held back from *Cowboys & Monsters,* either, as I did plenty of additional diggings to unearth more tales of the undead. Some of them I'm pleased to say I've never seen reprinted anywhere else, like a vampire attack in Brooklyn in the 1870s. Others may be familiar to you if you're a seasoned armchair vampire hunter. Those accounts I pilfered from excellent works like *American Vampires: Their True Bloody History From New York to California* and *New Orleans Vampires: History and Legend,* both of which I recommend you pick up if you enjoy this title.

Anyhow, if vampires are your favorite when it comes to creatures of the night, I hope this will prove to be one of the more thorough, unique books you've ever read when it comes to exploring the undead during North America's early days.

John LeMay
Summer 2022

CONTENTS

PREFACE   7

INTRODUCTION   11

CHAPTERS
1.	VAMPIRE HUNTERS OF EXETER	21
2.	VAMPIRE ON THE RANGE	31
3.	VAMPIRE WITCHES OF MEXICO	45
4.	SAINT GERMAINS IMMORTAL EXISTENCE	57
5.	THE VAMPIRE'S GHOST	67
6.	MYTH OF THE VAMPIRE TREE	75
7.	MINERAL POINT VAMPIRE	81
8.	TRIBE OF THE BAT PEOPLE	89
9.	THE VARNER VAMPIRE	95
10.	NEVADA'S VAMPIRE SKELETON	99
11.	MEXICAN VAMPIRE TREE	103
12.	LEGEND OF GREEN EYES	107
13.	VAMPIRE MEDICINE MAN	111
14.	VAMPIRE CHAIR OF TENNESSEE	119
15.	THE RICHMOND VAMPIRE	127
16.	PRESIDENTIAL PARDON FOR A VAMPIRE	135
17.	INTERVIEW WITH THE VAMPIRE'S VICTIM	143
18.	GREAT LAKES VAMPIRE PICTOGRAPH	149
19.	NOSFERATU IN NEW YORK	153
20.	THE VAMPIRE QUILT	161
21.	THE INVISIBLE VAMPIRE	165
22.	VANISHING VIRGINIA VAMPIRE	173
23.	BUCKET OF BLOOD	177

POSTSCRIPT: THE VAMPIRE'S GRAVE   181

INDEX 190

ABOUT THE AUTHOR 192

INTRODUCTION:
THE HISTORICAL VAMPIRE

As it stands, our perceptions of vampires stem more so from movies than from the real world. For most people, that stands to reason since vampires don't exist in the real world. Or do they? Historically speaking, vampires have been around since time immemorial. One of the very first stems from Adam's apocryphal first wife, Lillith. According to Jewish folklore, before Eve, there was Lillith. Long story short, Lillith was a bad girl and ended up becoming a vengeful spirit who subsisted on the blood of infants, some say as an act of vengeance against Adam's progeny.[1]

Vampire lore stems the strongest from Eastern Europe, though. When Austria took control of northern Serbia and Oltenia in 1718 via the Treaty

---

[1] Vampires have always served as a nifty excuse for misfortune. For instance, in Central America there is said to be a vampire witch that kills children on cold nights, a convenient excuse for anyone who accidentally let their baby freeze to death in the dark.

of Passarowitz, the new governing body was quite perplexed by a local custom wherein corpses were exhumed for fear of vampirism. Reports of this custom were widely published between 1725 and 1732. The term vampyre, as it was spelled back then, first surfaced in the English language that same year via reports of a vampire epidemic in eastern Europe.

Even amidst the so-called Age of Enlightenment throughout the 1800s, it seemed that belief in the vampire flourished more than ever. This was true of the peasants and the government officials alike when it came to vampire superstition. Innumerable graves were exhumed and stakes driven through corpse's hearts. The main outbreak began in East Prussia in 1721. Serbia, in particular, had a lot of vampiric resurrections, such as Miloš Čečar who was allegedly killed by a vampire on his farm and then rose again as one himself. Then there was Sava Savanović, who haunted a watermill and drank the blood of local millers. As incidents and bodies continued to pile up, government officials began to investigate, resulting in several official reports and entire books on the subject. Even before that, in 1597, King James himself mentioned vampires in his dissertation on witchcraft, *Daemonologie*, where he put forth the theory that demons could possess both the living and the dead.

Of course, it was Bram Stoker's seminal horror novel *Dracula* that cemented the vampire legend in the public consciousness. *Dracula* was itself predated by other works, most notably John

Polidori's *The Vampyre* in 1819. Following that was Sheridan Le Fanu's *Carmilla* in 1872.[2] *Dracula's* 1897 publication was the final nail in the coffin of the folkloric vampire. From thereon, vampires would be thought of as the Count in Stoker's world-famous work.

---

[2] Perhaps better known as Hammer's film version, *The Vampire Lovers*, from 1970.

DRACULA
By
Bram Stoker

And what you find in myth deviates significantly from *Dracula* and its many film adaptations. For instance, movies depict vampires as pale, frail creatures, while myth describes them as bloated, bronze-skinned beings. Instead of capes, many wore shrouds. Furthermore, vampires back then had decidedly ghostly traits, like turning invisible, throwing rocks at houses, and other specter-like behavior. And while the vampire always fed on blood, back in the old days, it wasn't just people at risk from the undead. Like today's better-known Chupacabra, many vampires back then attacked livestock.

In films such as *Horror of Dracula*, all that's needed to cure the vampire's current victim is to kill the vampire itself. Upon Dracula's death, Mina Harker reverts back to a normal human. Not so in folklore. Ever heard of cutting out the vampire's heart, burning it, and then having the victim drink the ashes? Such a remedy was actually tried in Exeter, Rhode Island, in 1892. And while many vampires the world over can be warded off by a crucifix, makeshift or otherwise, did you know you could immobilize others by taking your pants off and turning one leg inside out? Sillier still, you could throw some coins at an oncoming vampire in the hope that it would have to stop and count them per their obsessive-compulsive nature. In myth, many vampires, along with other supernatural beings, had the ability to turn into balls of light and streak through the air. This habit was never adapted to film, most likely, because special effects of the time would have found such a deed too difficult. Then, of course, there was the fact that Bram Stoker didn't adopt this trait for *Dracula*.

The idea of one becoming a vampire by another vampire's bite is also mostly the result of fiction. In Slavic and Chinese folklore, if an animal, especially a dog or cat, jumped over a dead body, it was thought it could become a vampire. Some vampires in Central America were believed to have been born that way. There was no reason for their condition, nor was there any cure. In some cases, it was believed that a body with a wound that had not been treated with boiling water could lead to vampirism.

In many myths the world over, vampires could be deceased witches, werewolves, or anyone who aligned themselves with the devil during life. A witch using blood magic could be considered a vampire. Or, a werewolf who drank blood, by default, could also be considered a vampire. Even some suicide victims were considered to be vampires after death. Possession could also make one a bloodsucker. Albanian folklore provided the most fantastic explanation for the birth of the vampire, that being that it was the offspring of a werewolf-like creature called the karkanxholl with a normal human. Or, if not the karkanxholl, the lugat, a water-dwelling monster of some sort, could be the non-human parent.

COWBOYS & VAMPIRES

How to prevent dead bodies from becoming vampires was also fascinating. Burying the body upside-down was common, in addition to placing scythes or sickles near the grave. The alleged undead might also be buried at a crossroads in hopes that they would become confused when they rose from the earth and not know which way to go. The Greeks would sometimes bury their dead with a wax cross and piece of pottery inscribed with the words "Jesus Christ conquers". More extreme methods from Europe had the dead's tendons severed at the knees in the hopes that they couldn't get up and walk again. Or, if they did, the locals would throw some sort of seed or grain along the ground. Due to the vampire's obsessive nature, it would have to stop and count them. To find a vampire's grave, the best method was to have a young man, still a virgin, ride a stallion, also a virgin, through the cemetery. The horse would then become agitated at the vampire's grave.[3]

After reading all that, you might be asking if *Dracula* and the movies got anything right at all? They did in the case of garlic being used to ward off vampires. In addition to garlic, a branch of wild rose or hawthorn can be implemented. Crosses and any type of Christian imagery will also do as in the movies. Holy water, of course, is also said to work. Furthermore, vampires are said to be unable to cross consecrated ground or running water, just as in the movies.

---

[3] If memory serves, the 1979 *Dracula* film had the bit about the horse, but not the virgin young man.

M. Michael Ranfts
Diaconi zu Nebra,

TRACTAT

von dem

Kauen und Schmaßen

der Todten

in Gräbern,

Worin die wahre Beschaffenheit
derer Hungarischen

VAMPYRS

und

Blut-Sauger

gezeigt,

Auch alle von dieser Materie bißher
zum Vorschein gekommene Schrifften
recensiret werden.

Leipzig, 1734.
Zu finden in Teubners Buchladen.

TREATISE ON "THE CHEWING AND
SMACKING OF THE DEAD IN GRAVES"
(1734), BY MICHAEL RANFT.

17

VAMPIRES & POSSESSION: A THEORY

If vampires are actually real, clearly they aren't like the ones presented in the movies. But what if they are real, and if so, what might they actually be? The Bible spoke of giants on the earth before and after the Great Flood. (Furthermore, the dreaded race of giants were the most notorious blood drinkers of the Bible.) According to the non-canonical Book of Enoch, the giants gave birth to demons when they died. Or, that is to say, that since the giants were hybrid combinations of angels and human women, when they died their souls could not enter Heaven, nor did they go to Hell. Instead, they were cursed to roam the earth. As such, is it any wonder that those who they possess crave human blood in some cases? Several of the accounts in this book point to possessed human beings with increased strength—a common attribute of possession—and a penchant for drinking their victim's blood. The act of blood drinking was typically attributed to demons in non-Biblical cultures as well. India had ghoulish beings that inhabited corpses called the vetālas, as did the Persians, who depicted bloodsucking demons on pottery.

The idea of a vampire not being able to show up in a mirror, made popular by *Dracula*, did not apply to vampire myths the world over. In many cases, the vampire simply abhorred seeing itself as opposed to not being able to see itself. The concept of sunlight being deadly to a vampire does come from *Dracula*, though. In real life, though vampires are believed to be more active at night, they are able to roam about in the sunlight.

THE UNDEAD IN NORTH AMERICA

The idea that a vampire cannot enter a house unless invited first possibly stems from similar theories dealing in demonology, the belief being that someone must invite the unwelcome spirit. Often this can happen unwittingly, by someone simply wearing a piece of jewelry inscribed with occult symbols or even watching a film where an occult ceremony is performed with accurate incantations. However, in a vampire's case, it's apparently a simple matter of the homeowner literally inviting them inside.

Destruction of a vampire was often done via the classic stake through the heart. However, there were alterations and additions not common to the movies. In Russia and parts of Germany, they were staked through the mouth, while in Serbia, it was the stomach. Ash was the wood of preference in many areas because it was believed Christ was crucified on an aspen cross. Likewise, placing aspen branches on a purported vampire's grave might keep them at bay for the night. Steel or iron stakes were also acceptable, not just in the heart, but even placed in the mouth during burial. In Bulgaria, over 100 skeletons have been found over the years impaled with some kind of metal object to keep the body from rising as a vampire. To be extra safe in Slavic areas the head was cut off and buried in between the feet. This was done in parts of Germany as well. And if one really wanted to go the extra mile, they would cremate the body. (This was not a popular Christian practice at the time, though, as it was thought the body could not be repaired on Resurrection Day if it had been incinerated.)

As neither *Dracula* nor its film adaptations like 1922's *Nosferatu* had yet to be released during the period that this tome covers, you'll notice that many of the vampires in this book correlate more so to folklore than film. In the interest of being objective, I would argue that only half of the cases presented indicate anything supernatural. Several I would chalk up to simple cases of possession where someone craved blood, though they weren't necessarily an immortal vampire. Of those, there are few, such as Comte St. Germain, which is the only one I think might actually be real. Many more, I think, are simply the product of local folklore that came about after movies made vampires popular. But, whether true or not, they all make for interesting reading, that's for sure!

CHAPTER 1
VAMPIRE HUNTERS OF EXETER

Today, when we think of vampires and their haunts, we think of dark Transylvanian forests and towering Romanian castles. This, of course, is thanks to the image of the vampire made popular by Bram Stoker in *Dracula,* published in 1897. Most people are aware that Stoker's vampire was inspired by the real-life figure of Vlad the Impaler, whose reign of terror took place during the 1400s. What most people don't know, though, was that Stoker was also inspired by a vampire story that came out of America in 1892. A real story, mind you, not fiction.

BELIEVE IN VAMPIRES.

Rhode Islanders Who Are Sure That They Do Exist.

Instances Told of Where the Living Have Been Attacked and Preyed Upon by These Representatives of an Unseen World.

A MEMBER OF THE ANTI-VAMPIRE PARTY.

In Exeter, Rhode Island, lived the family of George Brown. Over the years the clan suffered several deaths due to tuberculosis. As more and more family members died off, the superstitious townsfolk came to believe a vampire was to blame. They insisted that Geroge Brown's dead kin be exhumed, which Brown eventually agreed to. Two of the bodies—those being Brown's wife and one of his daughters—had decomposed at a natural rate.

JEWETT CITY VAMPIRES

Predating the Exeter, Rhode Island, case, but not as well-known was a similar but even more macabre event from Jewett City, Connecticut. From roughly the late 1840s into the early 1850s, the family of Henry and Lucy Ray were plagued by tuberculosis, still unidentified back then. First, Henry and his two oldest sons died of the condition, and in 1854, so did a third son. With four deaths in quick succession where the victims wasted away, a vampire was blamed. The remaining family then exhumed the bodies of the first two sons to die and burned them in the graveyard. The incident generated controversy in the papers but was largely forgotten for over a hundred years until the 1990s. Several children were playing along a hillside gravel mine in Jewett City when they found the long forgotten graves of the Jewett City Vampires as folklore now remembered them. And indeed, at least one of the graves was found to contain a body that had been burned. Not only that, the skull had been displaced from the body along with two femurs to make the famous skull and crossbones symbol, which was apparently an early day method of warding off vampires.

As such, they weren't counted among the undead. George's other daughter, Mercy, didn't appear to have decomposed at all. This wasn't because she was a vampire. It was simply because she had been buried in a freezer-like above-ground-crypt that preserved her body exceptionally well. The townsfolk didn't see it that way, though. They thought Mercy was a vampire and was responsible for her brother Edwin's worsening condition. (Again, he simply had tuberculosis.) Mercy's heart and liver were cut out and burned as per superstition. The ashes were then given to Edwin to drink! This was thought by the naïve townsfolk to be some sort of cure. It didn't work, and Edwin died only two months later.

The story made waves in 1892 and was resurrected five years later in several articles published in 1897. The one below offers one of the better accounts of the tale and comes from the September 19, 1897 edition of the *Cincinnati Commercial Tribune*:

THE HORRIBLE VAMPIRES

Rhode Islanders Who Believe in Their Existence And Go Upon Gruesome Hunts for the Alleged Blood-Sucking Ghosts—A Strong Belief.

That there exists in the thickly populated State of Rhode Island a community in which the people firmly believe in the vampire superstition and practice the rites which, early in the eighteenth century, were common among the Czechs of Bohemia is a curious ethnological fact. In the town of Exeter, almost within hearing of the scream of the railway whistle, graves are searched for the "vampire," and bodies or parts of bodies burned to save the living from his attacks. Along the line of the railways Rhode Island is thickly populated, and along the rivers and streams stretch for miles and miles continuous villages. But back of these densely populated regions one finds a lonely region, sparsely inhabited, and a primitive civilization. The world has not moved fast in those parts, and the minds of the inhabitants are still tinged with that mysticism which made their Puritan ancestors see signs and portents in the skies and burn witches at Salem. They are natural mystics, and their isolated lives foster the natural bent of their minds.

When a person falls sick of consumption, or some other wasting disease, from no apparent cause, the case is diagnosed by the old people of the community, who are expert in demonology, as being a case of vampire. They believe if the graves are searched, says the New York Press, there will be found a body, or some part of a body, full of blood and not yet gone to decay, and that in that body—generally that of a relative of the sick person, lives some essence of the dead person called "the vampire," which leaves the grave every night to suck the blood from the sick person. The way to effect a cure is this: The graveyards on the lonely hillsides must be searched, and when a body is exhumed which does not show the ordinary signs of decay the heart and liver must be examined to see if they are still full of blood, for it is in those parts that the vampire is supposed most commonly to have its dwelling place. Then the part filled with blood must be burned to kill the vampire. It is believed also that a part of the superstition is that the ashes of the burned parts must be given to the sick person in water in order to assure his recovery, but upon this part of their strange faith the vampire people keep a stolid silence. How often these vampire hunts are indulged in by the people of Exeter is not known to the outside world, but once in a while it is rumored about the countryside that "the vampire people are out searching the graves." Sometimes the news gets into the Rhode Island papers, and there is a mild sensation for a few days. The last vampire hunt which attracted attention was in 1892. A prosperous farmer was living with a family, consisting of his wife, two daughters and a son, all in good health. First the wife sickened and died of what the local doctor said was consumption. Then the daughters died, one after another, apparently of the same disease, and, lastly, the son began to waste away. He went to Colorado Springs, but, failing to get better, he returned to Exeter. Then all the neighbors assured the father that what was the matter with the young man was the vampire. Yielding to the opinion of the community, the father consented to a vampire hunt, and the medical officer of the district came by request from the neighboring village of Wickford to be present at it. The graves of the mother and the first daughter who had died were examined, and the bodies found to be little more than skeletons. But when the grave of the last daughter who had died was opened the body was found to be in an excellent state or preservation, though she had been dead over two months. The medical officer opened the body and took out the heart and liver. As the heart was lifted out, bright, red blood flowed from it, and the assembled people exclaimed, "The vampire!" A fire was then kindled near the graveyard and the heart and liver burned to ashes. The affair got into the Providence papers and was much talked of for a while.

About six years before this there was another vampire hunt in Exeter, news of which leaked out to the world. On that occasion it is said that a whole body was cremated, it having been discovered in its grave fresh and full of blood long after the usual period had elapsed in which bodies are expected to turn to dust.

The home of the vampire myth is in Slavonic lands. The word itself is of Servian origin, and means a blood-sucking ghost. Between 1790 and 1873 there was an outbreak of the superstition in Hungary, and from there it spread over all Europe. Some fringe of this wave of superstition must have broken upon the green and sparsely settled hills of Exeter, and as a receding wave upon the seashore will sometimes leave a little pool high upon the beach, so this wave of superstition left the vampire belief among the scattered farms or the ancestors of the present inhabitants of Exeter. The old things there do not change or give place to new, and the "vampire people" cling to the superstitions of their ancestors.

Aside from the people of Exeter, the only people among whom the vampire myth is still cherished are the Albanians and the people in some parts of rural Greece. The people of Exeter are not an irreligious people, and many of the farmers are well to do. Yet in all their religion and, in fact, in all their daily affairs, the strain of mysticism is ever present. They know what the outside world thinks of the vampire business, but they look upon the people of the outside world much as the Rev. Dr. Cotton Mather of pious memory looked upon those who did not believe in witchcraft. He said that the man who did not believe in witchcraft deserved to be burned himself.

The vampire myth in its wanderings over many lands from Hungary to find its last lodgment in a rural Rhode Island community suffered many changes of form. In Italy it was believed that living persons possessed the vampire gift, and simply by associating with a well person or exercising a certain will power on them could draw to themselves the life of the victim. When the time for the vampire to die was approaching he had to find a victim in order to prolong his life. In some cases the vampire was supposed to get the victim alone, murder him and suck the blood from the dead man's arteries. After that he had a new lease of life. It will be remembered that when Byron was living in Italy there was a certain Lord Ruthven, a pale, cadaverous man, living there, of whom the poet's friend, the beautiful Counteas Guicciolo, had a great horror, as he was believed by her and the Italian populace to be a vampire. But of all the stories that were ever written about vampires, none exceed in weirdness the story of the graveyard searches and cremations of the mystics on the lonely wind-swept hills of Exeter, just at our own doors.

DE MORAINE'S LITHOGRAPH
"THE VAMPIRE" C. 1864
DEPICTING A SCENE FROM EUROPE.

DRACULA AUTHOR BRAM STOKER.

Though it's not known which specific article exactly, one of the original 1892 accounts of the Mercy Brown incident was found in a scrapbook belonging to Bram Stoker. So, just remember, the next time that you're watching a Dracula movie, the Count's origins are staked here in America just as much as they are in Eastern Europe.

CHAPTER 2
VAMPIRE ON THE RANGE

In the spring of 1959, Universal Pictures, famous for their classic monster movies of the 1930s and 1940s, released their first vampire western. It was called *Curse of the Undead* and featured a typical Western plot device where the good guys and the bad guys feud over water and land rights. However, the black-clad gunman of this film turns out to be a vampire and is defeated by a gunslinging preacher with a special crucifix bullet. Supposedly the film was a hit at the box office but considering that hardly any more cowboys vs. vampire movies followed aside from 1966's ludicrous *Billy the Kid versus Dracula*, it couldn't have been that big of a hit.

POSTER FOR BILLY THE KID VS DRACULA

Oddly enough, the Old West has one literal cowboy vs. vampire tale up its sleeve, and no, it couldn't have been influenced by Bram Stoker's *Dracula.* This is because *Dracula* wasn't published until 1897, and this story appeared in newspapers in 1895. If anything, it might have been the other way around, and this story could have helped inspire *Dracula* considering that Stoker was known to keep a research notebook that contained a few newspaper clippings regarding vampirism in America.

Our fantastic tale, wherein a cowboy tussles with a genuine vampire in the vicinity of the Pine Ridge territory was published in the *Defiance Evening News* on November 12, 1895, and was still being ran as late as September 24, 1896, in papers across the country. Here is the story:

HUMAN VAMPIRE
Strangles Cattle With His Naked Hands.
HIS WONDERFUL STRENGTH
Attempts to Capture Him Prove Futile. No One Knows Who the Madman Is—Thrilling Experience of a Dakota Cowboy.

The cattlemen on the ranges west of Pierre, S.D., tell a ghastly story of a madman, who for some time past has been roaming over the reservation, killing cattle with his naked hands to suck their blood, and in some cases even attacking men. No one seems to know who the man is, nor how long he has been wandering about the ranges. He was first seen some four or five weeks ago. Repeated attempts have been made to capture him, but thus far without success.

He is said to labor under the hallucination that he is a vampire. How he manages without a weapon of any kind to kill the cattle on which he lives is a mystery. When found after he has left them the animals appear to have been seized by the heads, borne to the ground by main strength and torn to pieces by the teeth and nails of the lunatic.

Jack Lewis, a cowboy on one of the ranches about midway between Pierre and the Black Hills, is the hero of the most exciting adventure with the madman yet reported. It was nearly a fortnight ago. Lewis had been out for several days with a party on the range and about 6 o'clock in the evening he wandered away from his companions and dismounted for a few moments. As he stood by his horse he was suddenly struck from behind and hurled to the ground and nearly strangled by the maniac. He struggled furiously, but was unable to reach his weapon, while his assailant frothed at the mouth and made every effort to seize the cowboy by the throat with his teeth.

Such wonderful strength did he display that Lewis was nearly overpowered and would doubtless have been killed had not his friends, attracted by his cries, arrived in time to rescue him. The mad man flew when he saw this re-inforcement coming, and although pursued by several men on fast horses, he contrived to elude them in the dusk and made his escape. Lewis was quite badly torn about the face and neck by the man's teeth, and received a shock from which he has not yet fully recovered.

A few researchers have called this the first Chupacabra case. As all cryptid enthusiasts know, Chupacabras do suck the blood of livestock, though they are commonly described as looking like mangy coyotes rather than vampires. That said, I did find one other case of a male vampire feeding on cattle. It was published in the *Rushford Spectator* on August 14, 1884, on page two:

> The scene of another manifestation of the superstition which ended in a tragedy was laid in Hungary. A young miller, on the eve of his marriage with a peasant girl, was suddenly seized with a mortal illness, expired, and was burned the next day. That night several cattle were killed in a mysterious manner, and the young man's betrothed dreamed that she heard him calling for help. Her story, together with the incident of the dead cattle, inflamed the minds of the villagers, already saturated with the vampire belief. They repaired in a body to the miller's grave. On opening it the supposed corpse sat up with a loud cry. The mob cried vampire, and fell upon him immediately, and beat and mangled him with stones and clubs. A Physician who examined the body shortly afterward, declared it his opinion that the young man had awakened from a trance only to be murdered by his former friends.

A bit later, I stumbled across a more detailed version of the story that was printed in the *Columbus Daily Herald* on January 25, 1896. In the interest of being thorough—and also to give other researchers the full breadth of the case—I will reprint it below. However, if you are only interested in the highlights, I emboldened the notable differences.

HUMAN VAMPIRE'S DEEDS.

Strange Story of a Maniac Who Drinks the Blood of Cattle.

From out the wilds of Montana comes a strange story of a human vampire who seeks, slays and drains the blood of the cattle, **especially young calves.** Like the man-eating tiger, this strange being does not lacerate his victims, his only object seemingly being to suck their blood. Equally strange is the story current in the region infested by this monster. It is related that the man is an escaped lunatic, whose delusion is that he is a vampire and that his mission is to destroy animal life by draining the blood of all the victims his cunning or strength may place in his hands. **Carcasses of cattle and sheep have been found, but in no instance have they been disturbed beyond the slitting of the throat.**

The wild man, for he has been seen, is of superhuman strength, as there is evidence that he has caught and borne heavy steers to the ground unaided and has tore open the throat with his fingers or teeth, **he is said to be over six feet, of athletic build, and colored as darkly as an Indian, because of the exposure to the elements, he is entirely naked and possessed of marvelous speed.**

THE COWBOY WAS SEIZED FROM BEHIND

A cowboy on one of the ranches says he was awaiting the arrival of several of his party, from whom he had been separated for some time, and was resting himself by leaning up against the side of his horse. Suddenly he was seized from behind and thrown to the ground with such force as to almost deprive him of his senses.

A hand-to-hand struggle followed. The cowboy managed to hold out till the arrival of his companions, who were much closer than he had any reason to suppose. As soon as the lunatic caught sight of the other cowboys **he made a savage bite at the prostrate man's ear** and fled, the bullets from the guns of the party following him. So far as known the mad man was unhurt by the lead.

The vampire was first seen about a year ago. but when the story was told at that time there were few people who believed it, nearly all dismissing the story as the creation of someone who desired to start a sensation.

According to this story, the tale of the vampire started a year ago, as opposed to the later article, which stated it was over a month old. Nor is the cowboy's name given in this case. One article says he was torn about the face, while this one specifies that it was only his ear. Lastly, it claims the encounter took place in Montana rather than either Nebraska or South Dakota. When I initially began researching this story, I was a bit confused by the locations in which it allegedly took place. As it was, the article came from South Dakota, but it was Nebraska that really laid claim to the story. However, Nebraska is the south-bordering state of South Dakota. Together, South Dakota and Nebraska share an area known as the Pine Ridge Territory, which extends from Northern Nebraska into Southern South Dakota.

The official Nebraska history blog wrote that the story occurred in the "northwest county of Dawes,

107—"Vampire Peak", Cedar Pass. Bad Lands Nat'l Monument, So. Dak.

VAMPIRE PLACE NAMES IN SOUTH DAKOTA

Unrelated to our current tale, but interesting nonetheless, are a few noteworthy vampire place names in South Dakota. Vampire Peak was named in 1915 for the many bats in the area plus the blood red streaks of sand and rock that run across the peak. Then there is also Vampire Valley, though why it was named such is unknown.

[Nebraska] just around the Pine Ridge." Later it wrote that "There is a report of a Jack Lewis, a cowboy working ranches around the Black Hills [South Dakota] and northern Nebraska prairie, having a personal encounter with the vampire."

The author of the article, Nebraska State Historical Society Assistant Curator Dale Bacon, passed away in 2012, so I was unable to ask him whether or not any records proving Jack Lewis's existence were ever found. Likewise, I did my best to see if I could find records of Jack Lewis in the area myself. However, that's a fairly common name, which actually makes it harder rather than easier when it comes to ascertaining the validity of a story like this. Nor did the South Dakota Historical Society Press have any knowledge of this story at all when I asked.

However, just as I was ready to determine that this story was one of many one-off articles with no related tales or follow-ups, I found a potentially related account. This rare tale, often missed by many paranormal enthusiasts, was unearthed by the diligent researchers of strangehistory.net. The original story was published in the *Illustrated Police News* on April 25, 1895, along with the following illustration:

A VAMPIRE.

A wealthy rancher named Converse met a horrible death at Sioux City, Woodbury co. Iowa on Wednesday. There is a maniac confined in the Sioux City Lunatic Asylum who imagines himself a vampire, and is considered excessively dangerous. A close watch was kept over him, but he managed to elude the vigilance of the guards, and escaped on Wednesday morning. Not long afterwards he met Mr. Converse on the high road. He sprang at him in a fury, bore Converse to the ground, and literally tore him to pieces with his teeth. When Converse ceased to struggle the maniac fastened on his neck and sucked the blood from a gaping wound. He then returned to the asylum, where his shocking appearance showed the asylum officials that something dreadful had happened. Search was made, when the mangled body of the maniac's victim was discovered, mutilated almost beyond recognition.[4]

As it stands, Sioux City, Iowa, and the Pine Ridge region are roughly 350 miles apart. Could the vampire inmate of Sioux City have escaped again shortly after this article was published? And if he did, did he then flee to the Pine Ridge area where he resumed his reign of terror? The Sioux City account was published in April of 1895, and the Pine Ridge account was first published in November of 1895, giving the alleged vampire plenty of time to travel the open range.

---

[4] Although I was able to find this story a few different places, I would like to note that it was the user identified as "Beach Combing" who found the image from *The Illustrated Police News*.

A Human Vampire.

A WEALTHY rancher, named Converse, has met a horrible death at Sioux City, Iowa. There is a maniac confined in the Sioux City Lunatic Asylum who imagines himself a vampire, and is considered excessively dangerous. A close watch was kept over him, but he managed to elude the vigilence of his guards and escaped in the morning. Not long afterwards he met Mr. Converse on the high road. The maniac sprang at Mr. Converse in a fury, bore him to the ground, and literally tore him to pieces with his teeth. When Mr. Converse ceased to struggle the maniac fastened on his neck, and sucked the blood from a gaping wound. He then returned to the asylum, where his shocking appearance showed the asylum officials that something dreadful had happened. Search was made, when the mangled body of the maniac's victim was discovered mutilated almost beyond recognition.

However, that said, there's possibly a problem with the source of the Sioux City story. *The Illustrated Police News* from which it came was a tabloid as opposed to a respected news source. More than anything else, the goal of the paper was the exploitation of morbid crimes to shock readers. How much were these tales possibly embellished? Though based on real news items with lavish illustrations, it's tough to say how accurate their reports were. It was even voted the 'worst newspaper in England' by readers of the *Pall Mall Gazette*. That said, *The Illustrated Police News* is the first source of the story that we can find, but it could have appeared elsewhere first. For certain, it was afterward run in many newspapers in Australia, one of which was reprinted on the previous page.

As stated before, though the original source of the Iowa story is troubling, when placed in context with the better-known Nebraska tale, one has to wonder if a real vampire did ravage the ranges of the Midwest after all?

Sources:

Bacon, Dale. "Vampires of Nebraska." Nebraska State Historical Society. https://history.nebraska.gov/blog/vampires-nebraska

Beach Combing. "Iowa Vampire." Strangehistory.net. (December 28, 2017) http://www.strangehistory.net/2017/12/28/iowa-vampire/

CHAPTER 3
VAMPIRE WITCHES OF MEXICO

In the mid-1950s, rural Mexico was beset by a very unusual epidemic of infant deaths. They became so widespread in one particular region, the state of Tlaxcala, that it prompted a government investigation. This was because an alarming number of death certificates listed the cause of death as "*chupado por la bruja*" or, "sucked by the witch." The babies in question almost always died at night and were found with severe bruising or discoloration on their upper bodies. State authorities were sent to the capital city of the region, Tlaxcala City, to get to the bottom of the mystery. After all, it was the 20th Century, and the days of taking vampires and witches seriously were over long ago in most parts of the world.

Suspicious of the death certificates—and unable to prove whether or not vampire witches were indeed responsible—by 1954 the Mexican government decreed that any death certificate citing "*chupado por la bruja*" would be subject to an investigation. Basically, the government was suspicious that carelessness or negligence was to blame and hoped the fear of repercussions might curb the alarming rate of infant deaths. Did the Mexican government's ploy work? That's hard to say. Residents ceased listing "*chupado por la bruja*" as the cause of death most likely to keep the government out of their towns and villages, but the deaths still continued off and on in the region.

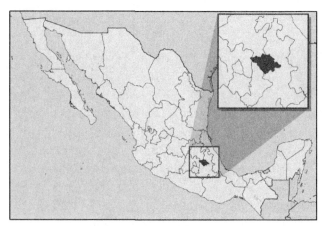

TLAXCALA REGION.

Tlaxcala is one of the smaller rural states of Central Mexico. The name itself dates all the way back to the pre-Conquest era in the form of a kingdom named Tlaxcala that had never formally joined the Aztec Empire despite sharing the same language and customs. The legend of the vampire witch, or Tlahuelpuchi, dates back to these times. The legend is unique to that locale and doesn't extend far outside of its confines. The myth always told of a shape-shifting vampire which subsisted on the blood of young infants, typically between two to ten months of age because the blood of a child that age was the most invigorating to them.[5] The myth of the tlahuelpuchi is quite different from typical vampire or werewolf lore in that these women are born that way, there is no occult ritual or vampire bite to transform them.[6]

The curse of the tlahuelpuchi is said to be irreversible and one will not even know that they are a vampire until puberty. Upon the tragic realization, the girl's soul is lost for several days as she becomes infused with special powers. These powers mostly include the ability to shapeshift into various animals, in this case those of a much smaller variety than we're usually accustomed to. Some tlahuelpuchi can even transform themselves into tiny insects and crawl their way through a keyhole to gain access to a home.

Most of the time, out of all the forms they could take, they choose that of the turkey. Not very scary compared to a wolf or a bat, but it is said that any animal the witch transforms into will generate a supernatural glow. It is through this glow that the creature can be tracked, and it is also where it

---

[5] Some say three to ten months instead.
[6] There can also be male tlahuelpuchi but they are very rare.

derives its name, coming from the Aztec word
tlahuia "to illuminate," thus tlahuelpuchi.[7] Perhaps
tying in to its luminescence are reports that the
tlahuelpuchi can also transform into fireballs,
which is common of witch folklore across the
southwestern U.S. as well. In addition to the glow,
the animal or person in question may also smell of
blood, albeit faintly.

Though the turkey is the most common form
that the witch takes, it will also take on others for
specific purposes. If she has a long way to go, she
will choose a bird capable of flight like a crow or
buzzard. If her house call is a short ways away, she
may only transform into a canine or a feline of
some sort, like a cat or coyote. However, she always
has to shapeshift into something that can fly when
she reaches the house. While the tlahuelpuchi
doesn't require an invitation to gain ingress to a
home, she does have to fly above it first in the
shape of a cross.[8] After that, she will sneak into the
house as an insect or a rat, and then return to her
turkey form oddly enough.

To keep the parents or older siblings asleep, she
will emit a supernatural mist that makes certain
they will not awaken as she feeds. As she
approaches the baby, she finally turns back into a
woman. Others say that she retains her turkey form
during the act, and sucks the blood through a long,
needle-like tongue. When she finishes, she will

---

[7] The name can also mean "fiery red smoke".
[8] Specifically, she must first fly east to west, and then north
to south according to some.

often leave the body outside of the crib or away from the sleeping mat, often near the door.

Supposedly the only ones able to resist the witch's sleep mist are shamans, and if one awakens and manages to ward off the witch, it is said she will return in the daylight hours to enact her revenge. At the very worst, she may put a spell on her prey that causes them to do self-harm, such as marching off a cliff. In less extreme cases, she may transform into a coyote or predatory animal to kill a family's livestock or even transform into a donkey to simply ruin newly planted crops.

The witch's method of transformation is also quite elaborate. On the last Saturday of the month, she will build a fire of dry zoapotl leaves, capulin wood, copal, and agave roots in her kitchen. While chanting, she will walk across the fire in the shape of a cross, north-south/east-west, three times before then sitting on the fire facing north, which enables her to enact the transformation. To reduce her size to that of the animal she wishes to emulate, she will remove her legs. Actually, that's perhaps more of a practical interpretation of the act. Folklore says that they do this because by removing their legs and losing the ability to walk upright, they lose what makes them human—perhaps drawing a parallel to the serpent in the garden forced to crawl upon its belly after tempting Adam and Eve.

Anyhow, when she separates from her legs, she often turns into a bird and flies away, and while she's out carousing, her legs sit in the kitchen. When she returns home, she sits on the fire again and begins to fit her legs back onto her body.

However, there will come a time when the tlahuelpuchi has done this too many times in her life and begins to look lopsided or walk with a limp. As such, unfortunately, elderly women who suffer naturally from these conditions may falsely be labeled as a witch. Other unfair correlations are made between the tlahuelpuchi and the obese, the thought being that they are overweight from consuming too much blood. And in traditional witch fashion, some elderly women are stereotyped as a tlahuelpuchi simply because they have long noses, squinty eyes, and squeaky voices.

As to other specific details concerning the tlahuelpuchi's habits, it is said to be most active during months that are either very cold or very wet. For instance, in the summer, they will usually feed during the rainy season, and in the winter will attack on the coldest nights.[9] In terms of when they will attack, anywhere between the hours of 12:00-3:00 AM is game. However, they do not require feeding every night, and supposedly only a few days out of the month will meet their needs. Furthermore, though rare, they will occasionally attack non-infants, like older children and adults, out of desperation, it is said. If they go without feeding altogether for one month, they will die. They will also die if they do not feed by daybreak when in their shapeshifted form.

---

[9] Some experts cite December, January, February, June, July, and August as the most common months due to the cold and rain respectively. However, from a practical perspective, these are also the nights most likely for an infant to freeze to death.

LAST RITES

The dead infants were often accorded special funerals usually seen over by a folk healer or priest with experience in warding off supernatural evil. Unlike other funerals, no music would be played and a cross made of pine ashes would be placed under the casket. After the burial, nearly all traces of the child were wiped clean. Their clothes are burned, no flowers are ever placed on their graves, and the child isn't even remembered on the Day of the Dead!

It is said that the witch's family is usually aware of her affliction and keeps it a secret since they believe the transformation was no fault of their own. However, there's another reason they won't out or kill a tlahuelpuchi within their family, that being that if they do, they will themselves turn into a vampire. By the same token, the tlahuelpuchi is incapable of killing their blood relatives or even relatives by marriage.

These vampire witches do not socialize or form covens with other witches and keep to themselves and occasionally fight over feeding grounds, it is said. However, some say that these witches will occasionally act as emissaries of the devil to negotiate occult dealings.

Warding off a tlahuelpuchi isn't completely dissimilar to a European vampire, as garlic is suggested in some cases, along with adorning the crib with Christian iconography and symbols. Though, being in Mexico, interestingly enough, they wrap the garlic—and sometimes onions—in a tortilla. As for religious symbols, some parents put the clothespins in the shape of a cross. Typically, though, the best way to protect a baby is to put a mirror in its crib as the tlahuelpuchi abhors mirrors and will shun them. Now, is this tied into the myth of the vampire casting no reflection? Not really. As it stands, the tlahuelpuchi abhors most any type of metal, reflective or not. In fact, they say the best repellent is a pair of scissors, a knife, a needle, or any other type of sharp metal left under the crib.

As to how one immobilizes a tlahuelpuchi, well, let's just say it wouldn't make for a very exciting ending to a movie. To do so, one can take off their pants, turn one leg inside out, and then throw the pants at the tlahuelpuchi. (Can't say I can imagine Professor Van Helsing ever doing that.) The other method, almost equally silly, is to place a rock within a white handkerchief and throw it at her. Lastly, if one is wearing a hat, they can remove it and place it upside down on the floor and then drive a knife through it. Any of these three methods will immobilize the creature, and afterward, it can be dispatched permanently. When it comes down to actually destroying a tlahuelpuchi, we get back into more exciting, normal territory, such as the good ol' fashioned stake through the heart or decapitation. The only unique method of killing one of these witches is to find their disembodied legs at the site of their kitchen fire and destroy them.

All that said, the only reported executions of a tlahuelpuchi that we know of didn't utilize any of these methods and consisted of the accused being stoned or clubbed to death like a normal human being. Afterward, their corpse was tossed into a ravine. Alternate reports indicate that other accused tlahuelpuchis were lynched, and their fingers and other sensory organs were cut off after death. The body would then be buried somewhere far away from the village. According to Mexico Unexplained, "many women in Tlaxcala have been killed for being suspected tlahuelpuchis."[10] The last known execution of a tlahuelpuchi occurred in 1973.

So, as you can see, stories of the tlahuelpuchi didn't cease in the mid-1950s. One of the more well-documented cases of a tlahuelpuchi occurred on December 8, 1960, again in the state of Tlaxcala. Specifically, it occurred in San Pedro Xolotla, a rural community in the vicinity of La Malintzi volcano. It was said to occur on an unusually cold night. Though several families were hit by the Tlahuelpuchi that night, the most documentation is afforded to a couple identified only as Filemón and Francisca, who lived in the home of Filemón's parents with their four children. They were in their early thirties, were primarily weavers, and had been working late carding wool and making yarn. Before turning in, Francisca breastfed her seven-month-old, Cristina, then put her on her sleeping mat for the night. Three hours later, Francisca awoke to a terrifying sight. A bright light was floating outside of her window. Similar to

---

[10] Bitto, "The Vampire Witches of Central Mexico," Mexico Unexplained. https://mexicounexplained.com/vampire-witches-central-mexico/

earlier reports of the tlahuelpuchi's ability to emit a sleep-inducing mist, try as she might, Francisca could not make herself get out of bed. Her body felt tired and heavy and so she fell asleep. Soon she woke again to find a mist filling her room and out of it formed a blue and red colored bird-like creature, said to resemble a chicken. That was her last memory before passing out again.

**SANCTUARY OF
OCOTLAN, TLAXCALA.**

The next morning at 6 AM, Filemón found baby Cristina dead. Not only that, she had been moved from her sleeping pad to the middle of the floor. As was typical with reports of the tlahuelpuchi, her chest and neck region were mottled and purplish in color, and her torso was covered in scratches.

THE UNDEAD IN NORTH AMERICA

THE LEMIA

You may have noticed some similarities to these infant killing vampire women to Lillith, mentioned in the introduction. The Greek had a very similar female vampire called the Lamia. It had a penchant for preying exclusively on children at night, and like the tlahuelpuchi, also liked to transform into birds. Having the body of a crow most of the time, it was later incorporated into Roman mythology as a strix, a blood drinking nocturnal bird.

That same morning, six other dead infants were found across the village, making for seven in total. Was it the tlahuelpuchi, or just the bitter cold that killed the babies? Though the latter seems more likely, why then did nearly all of the mothers report the same state of sleep paralyses? Were they ashamed that their babies froze to death in the night and used the tlahuelpuchi as an excuse, or did the shape-shifting witch actually pay them a visit?

Over the course of a decade, from 1959 to 1966, Hugo Nutini, future author of *Bloodsucking Witchcraft: An Epistemological Study of Anthropomorphic Supernaturalism in Rural Tlaxcala*, investigated the phenomena. In total, it is said he analyzed the deaths of 47 infants. Nutini observed,

> When traditional Tlaxcalans (which included almost everyone before 1960) verbalize the tlahuelpuchi complex, they are in fact presenting an explanation of why and under what conditions infants before the age of one

die, given specified circumstances.... It is almost as if by design that the accent of the ideology and belief system was place on explaining and rationalizing the death of infants as being beyond the control of the actors involved.[11]

Nutini himself examined a few of the deceased infants, as did a few doctors, all of which concluded that the babies had died of asphyxiation, not blood loss. However, no autopsies were performed, which makes the results inconclusive. When Nutini returned to the area in the mid-1980s, he found that hardly anyone used the term tlahuelpuchi anymore. The witch was quickly fading from modern folk belief into distant legend. Nor were infant fatality rates as high as they had been in the fifties and sixties and had been cut in half from 45% to only 20%.

Sources:

Bitto, Robert. "The Vampire Witches of Central Mexico." Mexico Unexplained (July 18, 2016)
https://mexicounexplained.com/vampire-witches-central-mexico/

Zumel, Nina. "The Tlahuelpuchi Epidemic." Multo Ghost. (September 10, 2015)
https://multoghost.wordpress.com/2015/09/10/the-tlahuelpuchi-epidemic

---

[11] Zumel, "The Tlahuelpuchi Epidemic," Multo Ghost.
https://multoghost.wordpress.com/2015/09/10/the-tlahuelpuchi-epidemic

CHAPTER 4
SAINT GERMAIN'S IMMORTAL EXISTENCE

Of all the cities in the U.S.A., New Orleans, Louisiana, is the one most associated with vampires—and not just because Anne Rice set her novel *Interview with the Vampire* there. One of the first vampire legends to emerge there was that of the vampiric "Casket Girls", who were supposedly held captive for over three centuries in the third-floor attic of the Ursuline Convent.

The legend began in 1727 and focused on a group of girls who sailed from France to New Orleans to go under the care of the Ursuline nuns before being given away in marriage to the many new male settlers there. Because the girls traveled with curious, coffin-shaped trousseaus as luggage, they were referred to as the casket girls. Supposedly, the girls had either knowingly or unknowingly smuggled vampires onboard the ship in their strange luggage. The vampires would sneak out at night to feed on the girls and members of the crew. Somehow, the Ursuline nuns were able to vanquish the vampires but felt too bad for the vampirized girls to kill them. And so, they locked them up in the third-story attic of the convent so that they couldn't do any harm. However, the legend is most likely just that, a legend made up long after the casket girls arrived.

NEW ORLEANS C. 1904

However, for a fact, late one night in 1903, a woman did claim to be attacked by a vampire in New Orleans. A party had just been held at the estate of wealthy socialite Jacques St. Germain at 1039 Royal Street. As several guests were leaving, a terrified woman fell from his balcony and landed nearby. The screaming woman, it was discovered, hadn't fallen by accident, she had jumped to escape the clutches of a vampire. The party-goers called for the police at once, as the girl, who it appeared might be a prostitute, continued her strange story.

She claimed that while she had been alone with Germain, he had bitten her on the neck. In between sobs, she said she only escaped because Germain had become distracted by a loud knock on the door.[12] At that point, the girl ran and jumped from the balcony, painfully breaking her legs in a few spots. When the police asked Germain about this, he passed it off on the woman being drunk. Since Germain was wealthy and respected, and the woman appeared to be a prostitute, her claims were not taken seriously. The woman was taken to a hospital, and the police asked Germain if he might come to the station the next morning to give a statement. When morning came, Germain never did. The police went to his home and found it deserted and Germain was never seen in New Orleans again.

If anyone ever fit the bill of a vampire, it was Jacques St. Germain, who had arrived in New Orleans the previous year. He was a mystery to those around him, always seen with a beautiful woman on his arm as he frequented fancy clubs

---

[12] An alternate version of the tale states that the girl was leaning over to gaze upon some beautiful items on Germain's mantle when he attacked her with superhuman speed and strength.

and enjoyed the New Orleans nightlife. What made him particularly enthralling were his stories, as Germain had apparently been everywhere. What made them odd was that Germain would speak of historical events from hundreds of years ago as though he had actually been there.

ROYAL STREET, NEW ORLEANS, AS IT WOULD HAVE APPEARED DURING ST. GERMAIN'S BRIEF REIGN OF TERROR.

What's more, Germain claimed to be the direct descendant of Comte de St. Germain, a close friend of King Louis XV who reigned from 1715 to 1774. People who compared the new St. Germain to his ancestor couldn't deny the resemblance was strong, and some even began to joke that the two were one and the same. And crazily enough, they may not have been wrong.

THE ENIGMATIC COMTE ST. GERMAIN.

Once stories began to spread about Germain's uncanny resemblance to his "ancestor", his party guests began to keep a more watchful eye on him. People began to whisper about how Germain was never actually seen eating at his parties. Not only that, he didn't seem to possess any silverware of his own, as it always belonged to the catering company. The only thing that Germain partook of was drink, presumably wine, from a lavish chalice.

Odder still, the original Comte de St. Germain even claimed in his day to be hundreds of years old! And, much as the "new" St. Germain had mysteriously arrived in New Orleans, Horace Walpole, the Fourth Earl of Oxford, also noted of Comte St. Germain's mysterious nature in a letter to Horace Mann:

> An odd man, who goes by the name of Comte St. Germain. He had been here these two years, and will not tell who he is, or whence, but professes that he does not go by his right name. He sings, plays on the violin wonderfully, composes, is mad, and not very sensible. He is called an Italian, a Spaniard, a Pole; a somebody that married a great fortune in Mexico, and ran away with her jewels to Constantinople, a priest, a fiddler, a vast nobleman. The Prince of Wales has had unsatiated curiosity about him, but in vain.

Supposedly, Germain refused to give his real name to anyone and only divulged it once to the King of France, Louis XV. Germain had arrived in France in 1756 bearing gifts that he hoped could aid the French economy. Specifically, he presented the French court with vibrant dyes to use in the creation of fabrics. There, Germain blatantly claimed to have partaken in historical events that took place as far back as 500 years ago. Among his bold claims were conversations with Cleopatra and even the Queen of Sheba. Though this sounds odd for someone to reveal, back then, people were more open-minded to the supernatural.

Whether or not he ever entertained the Pharaohs, Saint Germain was friends with the likes of Casanova, Catherine the Great, and Voltaire, who called him "a man who never dies, and who knows everything." Once, in 1760 at the home of King Louis XV's mistress, Countess von Gregory told Germain that he looked like someone she had met 50 years ago. The resemblance was so strong that she assumed Germain to be his son. Instead, Germain joked that he was over 100 years old! As they say, sometimes the best way to hide is in plain sight.

Stories alleged that Germain was part of the council of Nicaea in 325 A.D., which helped shape Christianity as we know it. More shocking still, some even claimed Germain was at the wedding at Cana where Jesus turned water into wine. Germain had many miraculous talents himself, including being ambidextrous and an esteemed linguist, alchemist, and musician. Supposedly he could precipitate diamonds from thin air and change stones into jewels. He could supposedly also manipulate metal into gold.

According to the history books, Comte St. Germain died on February 27, 1784, at the castle of Prince Charles of Hesse-Cassel. However, Germain was still sighted after his death, notably at the execution of Marie Antoinette in 1793. He was seen several times before arriving in New Orleans as well.

**CAGLIOSTRO, A MYSTIC
SIMILAR TO ST. GERMAIN.**

After the New Orleans incident, St. Germain was
next sighted in Rome in 1926 by Freemason C. W.
Leadbeater, who claimed that Germain told him
that he currently lived in a castle in Transylvania.[13]
In his book, *The Masters and the Path*, Leadbeater
claimed that Germain told him that when

---

[13] Though no official birth records for Germain can be
found, in her book *The Comte de St. Germain, the Secret of Kings*,
Isabel Cooper-Oakly suggests that he was the youngest son
of Prince Franz-Leopold Rakoczy of Transylvania! However,
this is simply her educated speculation, not fact. In any case,
it provides yet another link to the alleged vampire and
Transylvania.

CAGLIOSTRO AND ST. GERMAIN

As opposed to being a vampire, some alleged instead that St. Germain had unraveled the secrets of transmutation via alchemy. This is similar to tales of the Italian mystic Cagliostro. Born Giuseppe Balsamo in 1743, the Italian occultist took on the alias of Count Allesandro Di Cagliostro. Oddly enough, this man was the inspiration behind Universal Studio's famous Mummy franchise, which began with *The Mummy* in 1932. However, that film was initially called *Cagliostro, King of the Dead.*

This is because, even though Cagliostro wasn't Egyptian, he spent several years in Egypt studying Egyptian mysticism. The enigmatic mystic claimed that he was 3,000 years old, among other things, and in 1777 he founded the Egyptian Rite of Freemasonry. By 1785, his home was ornately decorated with Egyptian symbols and his servants dressed in Egyptian robes. In 1789 he was arrested as part of the Inquisition and thrown in jail where he died... or did he? According to legend, he didn't die as no body was ever found. He simply disappeared from his cell.

Not coincidentally, it is rumored that Count Alessandro di Cagliostro met Comte de Saint-Germain. If this is true, then perhaps the two compared notes on immortality formulas? Furthermore, elite occultists have for years held that blood is the key to eternal youth, so perhaps the truth is a conflagration of both the alchemist and the vampire idea.

performing magical rituals in his castle that Germain wore "a suit of golden chain-mail which once belonged to a Roman Emperor; over it is thrown a magnificent cloak of Tyrian purple, with on its clasp a seven-pointed star in diamond and amethyst, and sometimes he wears a glorious robe of violet."

St. Germain next appeared rather appropriately on California's mystical Mount Shasta in 1930. Even in the current century in which we live, people still occasionally claim to see him.

But was—or should we say is?—Germain really a vampire? I'll leave you with this. When the police went to his home the morning after the famous incident in New Orleans, even though they found no trace of Germain, when searching through the drawers, they found blood-stained tablecloths that appeared to have accumulated over the various parties. And as guests had always suspected, not a piece of silverware was found within the house. Lastly were found wine bottles filled with a mixture of wine and human blood...

Sources:

Crandle, Marita Woywod. *New Orleans Vampires: History and Legend.* The History Press, 2008.

Swancer, Brent. "A Real Immortal Vampire in New Orleans." Mysterious Universe (July 26, 2018). https://mysteriousuniverse.org/2018/07/a-real-immortal-vampire-in-new-orleans/

CHAPTER 5
THE
VAMPIRE'S
GHOST

Our next tale centers around the Slagle Cemetery of Livingston County, Missouri. The cemetery was named for Joseph Slagle, who arrived in the area from West Virginia around the year 1830. He would have been twenty years old at the time and had previously studied for the ministry. At an unspecified point in his life, he also lost one of his arms, giving him a rather distinct characteristic. By 1839, he was a store clerk at Cox's Mill in Medicine Creek. Eventually, he bought the mill and worked his way up to Justice of the Peace and was even elected to the County Bench in 1846. As his interests grew, he became one of the largest landowners in the area.

 Slagle was controversial in his era for having been married five times already, each of the wives dying mysteriously. A whole book has even been devoted to Slagle: *The Four Consorts of Joseph Slagle, An Unauthorized Biography of Judge Joseph Slagle* by Gary Thomas, who notes that Slagle "was also known for creating a private burying ground, surrounded by a high brick wall, that is said to be haunted by the spirits of his four brides – seemingly healthy young women who died inexplicably and were buried without ceremony. Yet, no one stepped forward, fearing they, too, might suffer grave consequences."[14]

The first, Catherine Long, lasted as his wife from 1832 to 1841 when she died of unknown causes, right around the same time that it was rumored Slagle was already seeing someone else. In November of 1843, Slagle was hitched again, this time to Catherine Stone of West Virginia. She lasted just short of a year, passing in August of 1844. By May of the following year, Slagle was married again to Sarah Littlepage, who made it over a year into September of 1846. Unlike the other two wives, Slagle had a daughter with her (unless she came from a previous marriage) named Susan Catherine.

---

[14] Mouton, "Book pieces together 175-year-old mysteries surrounding Judge Joseph Slagle," Lubbock Online.
www.lubbockonline.com/story/news/2018/06/12/book-pieces-together-175-year/11992357007/

And just how and where did Slagle get all of these wives? Author Mary Saale conducted interviews with Livingston County residents in November of 1979 to dig up some answers. According to Mr. Howard Wray Leech, the source of his many brides was a crossing spot at the river. Leech explained:

> See, this was a crossing of the river there where he had his mill and that was on the trail of people going west from Indiana and Ohio and Illinois, and they would have these young ladies in their personnel of people that were making this trip and ... that was his source of supplies for his wives--those young ladies in those caravans that were going west.[15]

Eunice Inman, another interview subject, also corroborated this, stating, "I was told that when he lost a wife he would always go back to Ohio for his next wife. He didn't marry into the young women around here."[16]

And how did Slagle kill these women? Many said he either hung, choked or poisoned them once he grew tired of them. One interviewee stated, "They said he hung one, choked one, pushed one down the stairs and poisoned all the rest." However, even more macabre rumors than that existed...

---

[15] Saale, "The Legend of Slagle's Mill," Livingston County Library. www.livingstoncountylibrary.org/History/Places/Mills/slaglemill1.htm

[16] Ibid.

Slagle wed again in 1848 to Elizabeth Crawford of Illinois, who was a goner by the start of 1849. Naturally, townspeople began to talk, stating that Slagle murdered the women to inherit their money. Others had darker theories, those being that Slagle had been expelled from the ministry for selling his soul to the devil. As such, his poor wives had become sinister sacrifices. These rumors reached the ears of Elizabeth Crawford's half-brother, Benjamin Collins. Elizabeth had yet to die by then, and Collins was determined to see to it that she didn't end up as another macabre sacrifice.

Collins made a fatal mistake in boasting of his plans to the community, that being to slay the monstrous Slagle. Naturally, Slagle learned of this. So the story goes, Slagle had a chance meeting with Collins while he was out searching for a lost cow. Since it wasn't unusual for a man to be armed with a rifle on the prairie, Slagle basically shot Collins on sight. When the case went to trial, Slagle was acquitted on the basis that Collins had stated he intended to kill Slagle. Others say the trial was rigged to let Slagle off. After that close call, Slagle waited twenty years before taking another wife, that being Miss Lottie P. Ellis of Indiana in 1869. She bore him a son, Joseph Lee Slagle. This was apparently Slagle's final marriage, and he died in 1895. The cemetery became known as Slagle Cemetery due to so many of Slagle's wives being buried in it, not to mention Slagle himself!

And this is where the tale finally turns vampiric, though not in the way that you might expect. Before we get into it, it's important to note that in the old days, many supernatural entities—be they werewolves, witches, or vampires—could turn into orbs of light and fly. (This was never adapted into movies because special effects back then weren't sophisticated enough to pull that off most likely, and thus that aspect of supernatural creatures faded into obscurity.) In the case of Slagle Cemetery, passers-by claim to sometimes see a terrifying ghost light that leaves them drained of energy. Stranger still, sometimes the face of Joseph Slagle could be glimpsed within the orb of light.

Eunice Inman related another tidbit about the haunted cemetery as well when asked if it was haunted. She stated that ten years ago, which would have been the late 1960s, a woman came into the beauty shop and claimed that she and her boyfriend had a haunted encounter there. Eunice said that the couple was

> ...sitting there parked and it was a warm evening and they had the windows rolled down and she was leaning back towards her car door and they were talking and all at once she felt some unseen hands come into the window and go around her neck like this [Informant demonstrates] and then in a little while he felt a hand on his side come in around his neck and they just knew it was haunted.[17]

As for more cemetery encounters, other residents said there was a tradition that if you

----

[17] Ibid.

knocked on Slagle's grave on Friday the 13th, he would knock back. Another rumor stated that the brides would emerge from their graves to wander the cemetery as they wept. A woman named Ruth recollected that,

> One night I went out there with some friends because we heard his wives came out of their graves and walked around the cemetery weeping. The cemetery was pretty grown up with brush and it was real dark that night. We walked to the gate all of a sudden we saw the brush moving on the other side of the cemetery. We didn't wait around to see what is was. It could have been some sort of animal, but if it

wasn't we didn't want to mess around with the dead.[18]

In addition to the cemetery, a nearby bridge was also haunted by the vampiric ghost light. Actually, whether one saw the light or not, many who crossed the bridge reported feeling lethargic for several hours after. The same went for an abandoned mill in the area. Tales of devil lights dated all the way back to the times of the missionaries, specifically a Father Marquet. On the banks of the Mississippi River, some Native Americans pointed to some hills in the distance and claimed that from them emerged ghostly lights that sucked the energy out of a person.

Actually, according to one witness identified as Eunice, it is possible that Slagle himself witnessed the ghost lights. Unfortunately, Eunice's statement is vague, but she said that,

> My Great-Grandfather Wilson on my mother's side was a friend of Mr. Slagle's and my great-grandfather would say that he would be walking with Mr. Slagle, say cutting across the pasture and Mr. Slagle would look back and say, "See, there she comes, there's that ghost."[19]

In all likelihood, the mysterious deeds of Joseph Slagle were merely conflated with the ghost light sightings already native to the area. Therefore, the

---

[18] Ibid.
[19] Ibid.

ghost lights that were already there in Slagle's time were made to become his vampiric ghost.

Sources:

Curran, Dr. Bob and Ian Daniels. *American Vampires: Their True Bloody History From New York to California.* Weiser (October 22, 2012)

Mouton, Kirsten. "Book pieces together 175-year-old mysteries surrounding Judge Joseph Slagle." Lubbock Online. (June 12, 2018)
www.lubbockonline.com/story/news/2018/06/12/book-pieces-together-175-year/11992357007/

Saale, Mary. "The Legend of Slagle's Mill: A Collection by Mary Saale." Livingston County Library. (November 26, 1979)
https://www.livingstoncountylibrary.org/History/Places/Mills/slaglemill1.htm

CHAPTER 6
MYTH OF THE VAMPIRE TREE

According to local lore, buried in the municipal cemetery of Lafayette, Colorado, is a vampire who died in 1919. People claim that the grave is the site of much paranormal activity with spectral figures seen hanging about along with disembodied voices and strange lights. People have also claimed to have been attacked by a mysterious figure, and the only clues are a set of footprints leading back to the grave. And one of the strangest details of all: battery operated devices quickly become drained in the grave's vicinity.

And why the furor over the grave? There are two reasons. The man buried there was from

Transylvania, and, also, a large tree grows from right where the man's chest would be. According to the legend, the tree grew from a stake driven through the man's heart. And why did he have a stake driven through his heart? Well, he was a vampire, of course! According to the legend, for reasons unknown, the townsfolk dug up the man's remains shortly after his burial. They saw that the man had blood near his mouth, which contained larger than normal teeth. To top it off, the man also had extremely long fingernails. And so, the townsfolk did the sensible thing and drove the aforementioned stake through his heart.

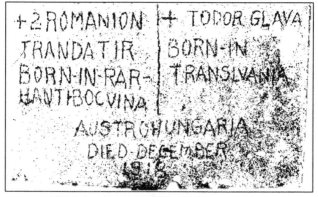

THE LAFAYETTE HEADSTONE.

Actually, two men are buried in the grave, as was sometimes the custom back then. The first man was Todor Glava, an immigrant from Austria (but born in Transylvania) who died on December 6, 1918, most likely from influenza due to the 1918 pandemic. The second man was John Trandafir, also of Transylvania, who died about a week later on the 13th. His cause of death had nothing to do with vampire lore either. (In other words, no holy water, decapitation, or stakes to the heart.) Probably also due to the 1918 pandemic, Trandafir died of pneumonia. Of the two men, it was Todor Glava who was thought to be the vampire.

LAFAYETTE, COLORADO, C.1920s.
(LAFAYETTE HISTORICAL SOCIETY)

Lafayette had been a booming mining town back in the late 1800s and early 20th Century. As such, it attracted many immigrants looking for work. When asked about the alleged vampire, Claudia Lund, curator of the Lafayette Miner's Museum, said, "Supposedly [he was] a miner that came from Transylvania. And that part of the world has always had a certain history behind it. Particularly the Dracula story and everything."[20]

---

[20] "There's a vampire buried in Lafayette?" (KUSA, 2015)
https://www.9news.com/article/news/theres-a-vampire-buried-in-lafayette/134429175

COWBOYS & VAMPIRES

As it stands, there are no stories of either Trandafir or Glava attacking the populace of Lafayette. The vampire legend sprang about predominantly from the tree apparently.[21] "A tree, supposedly, mysteriously grew up from the grave where his heart would have been, and people wondered if there wasn't a stake driven through his heart because they thought he was a vampire," Lund explained.[22] When blood-red roses also grew near the grave (said to be his fingernails), that was apparently all people needed to start the vampire story.

After the vampire myth was established, local children would dare each other to stand upon the grave as children do. It wasn't long after that stories started to emerge about ghosts being sighted near the grave along with strange voices being heard. One investigator, Anam Paranormal, took an EVP (electronic voice phenomena) device to record the noises near the grave and also an EMF, which detects electromagnetic fields. The results were surprising.

Anam Paranormal recorded that, "EMF ranged from zeros to maxes and never really stayed at one reading or another the whole time, so good luck getting a decent base reading for comparison. Even in the daytime, EMF went too nutty." Spookier

---

[21] I would guess that the tree came first, and the legend of locals staking the dead man in his grave came after.
[22] "There's a vampire buried in Lafayette?" (KUSA, 2015)
https://www.9news.com/article/news/theres-a-vampire-buried-in-lafayette/134429175

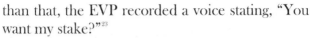

than that, the EVP recorded a voice stating, "You want my stake?"[23]

However, Anam Paranormal doesn't believe that the spirit residing near the grave is an actual vampire, but rather a ghost playing off the grave's reputation. An interesting theory for certain.

Sources:

Anam Paranormal. "114 - Lafeyette Cemetery - The Vampire Grave." https://www.anamparanormal.com/114

KUSA Staff. "There's a vampire buried in Lafayette?" (KUSA, 2015) https://www.9news.com/article/news/theres-a-vampire-buried-in-lafayette/134429175

---

23 https://www.anamparanormal.com/114

CHAPTER 7
MINERAL
POINT
VAMPIRE

For most people, the tale of the Mineral Point Vampire begins on March 14, 1981. On that night, police responded to reports of a strange looking man haunting the Graceland Cemetery. According to the witness testimony of officer John Pepper, he saw what he described as "a huge person, wearing a black cape with a white painted face...... about 6' 5" and ugly." Or, in other words, Pepper encountered a classic vampire from a Hollywood horror movie from the days of Bela Lugosi and Christopher Lee. When the officer asked the vampiric-looking man what he was doing in the cemetery, the man turned and ran. Pepper was never able to catch the vampire and watched as it cleared a four-foot fence and ran into an adjacent cow pasture where Angus bulls were grazing. After the report went public, the Wisconsin town of Mineral Point went wild with rumors of a vampire. As winter turned to spring, sightings of the vampire man continued. After that flap of sightings dissipated, they resumed over twenty years later in the early 2000s with more vampire sightings.

The most terrifying sighting of all occurred along a jetty in 2008. A pair of young lovers were fishing at Ludden Lake when they heard something crawling underneath the jetty they were fishing on. When the young man aimed his flashlight at the boards beneath their feet, he spied the same pale-faced vampire man sighted back in the 1980s crawling underneath! The couple ran to their car with the caped creature in hot pursuit and they fled the area.

As an old mining settlement with Cornish roots, Mineral Point is an appropriate home for a vampire. And, as it turns out, the vampire had been lurking for much longer than initially thought, and sightings had begun back in the mid-1800s when it was known under the name of the Ridgeway Phantom. (Ridgeway is an area located between Mineral Point and Blue Mounds, by the way, so it's not far.)

Ridgeway sported a variety of paranormal activity including headless ghosts and spook lights but the most famous was always the Ridgeway Phantom. It liked to prey on lone travelers in the woodlands late at night—but then again, don't they always?

More specifically, the Ridgeway Phantom haunted what was called the old Military Road nearest the aptly named town of Pokerville in Iowa County. It haunted a 25-foot stretch of the road that spanned from Pokerville to Dodgeville, both of which were mining communities just like nearby Mineral Point.

REMAINS OF RIDGEWAY.

The area boasted no less than a dozen saloons, if not more. Ridgeway, in particular, was a wild spot with numerous fights, robberies, and murders in the area. For some reason, locals tied the origins of the Ridgeway Phantom to the murder of two teenage boys at McKillip's Saloon in 1840. The boys' names have been lost to history, but they were aged fourteen and fifteen. The younger of the two was tossed into a fireplace for reasons unknown by some evil saloon goers, while the other froze to death outside as he fled town. The boys had died by fire and ice, and somehow, someway, the Ridgeway Phantom arose from the killings and began to haunt the area soon after. Rather than looking at the different ghosts as separate entities, local lore said they were all the shapeshifting phantom. That's how the more recent Mineral Point Vampire ties in, as folks seem to think that it's the Ridgeway Phantom's modern form. And he could be if we follow the John Keel school of ultraterrestrials.

You most likely don't need a refresher on Mothman, but you're getting one anyways. As you may recall, in 1967, Point Pleasant, West Virginia, was besieged not just by the strange, winged humanoid known as Mothman, but also ghosts, UFOs, and the Men in Black all at once. Due to this, Keel began to speculate that Mothman and his kin might be a form of the older trickster myth, a being beyond our understanding that either couldn't or wouldn't communicate in a normal way. He dubbed these modern era tricksters "ultraterrestrials", the idea being that these neo-tricksters shapeshifted into a form that a witness of the era would recognize. For instance, in 19th century Ireland, ultraterrestrials might take the form of fairies, while in 20th century America they might appear as aliens and so on. So perhaps the trickster of Iowa County, Wisconsin, took on various forms over the years, starting with the spook known as the Ridgeway Phantom and eventually gave itself a makeover into something more akin to a Hollywood vampire.

And indeed, the being did have the behavior of a trickster all the way back in the mid-19th century. The website The W-Files wrote of the specter that,

> He ranged the Highway and the surrounding farmlands, playing his mischievous and harmful pranks upon travelers and inhabitants alike. He was that most exasperating of phantoms, the practical joker, and one who shamelessly exploited his obvious advantage, played according to no rules whatever, and generally turned out to be a downright nuisance.[24]

For instance, according to lore, the invisible specter joined in one of Pokerville's many poker games one night. Three miners sat playing poker, with a fourth chair left empty, and you can guess what invisible figure was really sitting in it. When one of the men won a full pot and went to grab his winnings, the cards suddenly began to shuffle themselves for the next round as though by invisible hands. Suddenly, a strange man materialized in the fourth seat, his hat pulled down partly over his face to conceal it.

The men let the stranger play with them, only odd things happened to the cards he dealt. After picking up a card, it would instantly leave the person's hand and fly around the room! Soon, a

---

[24] http://www.w-files.com/files/ghridgeway.html.

whole slew of cards was flying around the table in a circle, and the miners ran out the door.

There were several occasions where the ghost lashed people with a switch. One night two Pokerville men were carrying a plank across their shoulders down the road. A being dressed in all white suddenly leaped from the bushes, landed on the plank, and began whipping the men with a switch. They ran, and eventually the being disappeared.

In another incident, a man named John Riley was preparing to take his wagon down the old Military Road. Afraid of the ghost, he went inside to get a drink to muster his courage. When he returned, his oxen had suddenly been hitched to the rear of his wagon. In the distance, he could see what he knew to be the ghost walking away—a trickster indeed. After a while, all the area's misfortunes were blamed on the Ridgeway Phantom. These are just a few of the tales to concern the specter, which could probably fill a book of their own.

According to at least one source, the Ridgeway Phantom was seen in flaps about forty years apart, starting in the 1840s, resuming again in the 1890s, 1930s, and 1970s. The Mineral Point Vampire seems a bit more impatient, as it popped up every ten years for a while as opposed to every forty. But what purpose do these strange ultraterrestrials serve? Do they just enjoy pranking the more primitive human race, or is there something more behind their seemingly random appearances? John Keel holds that ultraterrestrials served as omens preceding disaster. In Mothman's case, there was the Silver Bridge collapse. In South America, a glowing "terror bird" preceded a great earthquake in Peru in 1868. So far as we can tell, the Ridgeway Phantom never preceded any major catastrophes or natural disasters, but those from the Keel school of ultraterrestrials did point out that the first sighting of the Mineral Point Vampire in mid-March of 1981 preceded the assassination attempt on President Ronald Reagan later that month. Coincidence? Perhaps, but until the mystery of these spooks and so-called ultraterrestrials is solved, every bit of information serves as a potential piece of the puzzle.

Sources:

Hauck, Dennis William. *The National Directory Of Haunted Places*. Penguin Books, 2002.

NORTH CAROLINA EFFIGY WITHIN THE CHEROKEE COUNTY HISTORICAL MUSEUM.

CHAPTER 8
TRIBE OF THE BAT PEOPLE

Since vampires are so heavily linked to bats, it seems appropriate then to discuss a mysterious tribe from North America's past that had several bat-like attributes.[25] They were called the Moon-Eyed People by other Native American tribes and were reported across the Southeastern United States. Thomas Jefferson even mentioned the Moon-Eyed People in his Indian Removal Act of 1803.

We'll begin our tale of the Moon-Eyed People with the discovery of a strange stone effigy. It was

---

[25] Full disclosure, I have written on this tribe before under the guise of ufology and aliens, but as their origins are certainly mysterious and unknown, I thought I might take a stab at them from the vampire angle as well.

unearthed in Murphy, North Carolina, as the land was being cleared by a farmer in the 1840s. The stone statue appears as though it's supposed to be a life-sized representation of two three-foot-tall beings conjoined like Siamese Twins. Furthermore, they have dished-in faces, no arms, and very big, round eyes. There are many theories as to what the beings might be, but the most prevalent is that they represent the Moon-Eyed People.[26] Quasi-similar effigies were found at a large mound in Williamson County, Tennessee. Illustrations of the figures and the record of their discovery was published in the 1876 article "Explorations of the Aboriginal Remains of Tennessee" by Joseph Jones.

But who were these Moon-Eyed People, and why were they so controversial? Folklore says that they were nocturnal like bats, coming out to hunt only at night, preferably by the light of the moon. Their eyes were larger than normal humans and very round at that. Their sight was also quite weak in the daylight, and their skin was pale from shunning the sunlight. Like bats, they were even said to live underground. The Moon-Eyed People were regarded as extremely dangerous by some and as incredibly weak by others.

Supposedly, they made their way to the surface by following underground rivers and sinkholes until they met the surface. Native American lore

---

[26] However, in the interest of being thorough, some think that they are meant to be depiction of the "Little People" common to most Native American myths.

mentions spirits living within the wells and the waters that could syphon off a person's energy like a vampire. According to some accounts, the Moon-Eyed people would occasionally attack camps at night and drink their victims' blood. However, that's the more extreme cases of folklore, and the written record defies the Moon-Eyed People's fierce nature.

The first mention of the Moon-Eyed People may have come from a conquistador, Alvaro Nunez, who mentioned them in his writings. Nunez, who was part of the Narvaez expedition which landed in Florida in 1528, recalled:

> Some of the Indians brought many people before us, the greater part whereof were squint-eyed, and others of the same people were blind, whereat we greatly marveled. They [were] well-set and of good behavior, and whiter than all the rest that we had seen until then.

Though that description is rather vague, later descriptions were more detailed and much more interesting. We will begin with the variety of Moon-Eyed People encountered in Tennessee and Kentucky, as they are the most interesting. They were said to be small in stature, pale white or albino, flat-faced, and had huge eyes with blue irises. In accordance with stories of the Moon-Eyed People living underground, many written accounts identified them as mound dwellers, though they were also said to live in caves and other dark, subterranean places. An alternate report states that rather than living underground due to an abhorrence of the sun, it would seem the Moon-Eyed People were driven to caves by hostile tribes and, before this, lived in stone houses which were fairly advanced in their construction.

Benjamin Smith Barton's 1798 book *New Views of the Origins of the Tribes and Nations of America* makes mention of the race of strange people. According to the book, the Cherokee claimed that when they first came to Tennessee that they came upon a strange tribe of highly advanced white men fitting the description of the Moon-Eyed People. They lived in stone houses and were nocturnal, unable to stand sunlight. The Cherokee could not understand their language, and to them it sounded like gibberish. Despite their advancement in terms of architecture, the Cherokee nonetheless considered these strange people inferior due to their inability to communicate and drove them from the area.

Specifically, Barton quoted a Colonel Leonard Marbury who reported that "the Cheerake [sic] tell us, that when they first arrived in the country which they inhabit, they found it possessed by certain 'moon-eyed-people,' who could not see in the day-time. These wretches they expelled."

Supposedly, after their expulsion into the wilderness, the Moon-Eyed People built the semi-famous mounds of Tennessee. The Moon-Eyed People were mentioned again in the 1824 writings of John Haywood, who claimed that the Cherokees had discovered a tribe of bug-eyed white men living near the mouth of the Little Tennessee River. The tribe had built forts of stone all the way down to Chickamauga Creek.[27]

Tales of the Moon-Eyed People can also be found in the Ohio River Valley. A battle between a local Native American tribe and the Moon-Eyed People took place at the Falls of the Ohio River near present-day Louisville, Kentucky. All of the Moon-Eyed People were allegedly killed on an island below the falls. Years later, settlers reported finding a large cache of human bones there.

Traces of the Moon-Eyed People were also found in Cherokee County, North Carolina. According to the Native Americans, the Moon-Eyed People were the area's first residents and pre-dated even their creation myths.

Some historians have put forth the theory that the mysterious mound builders of North America were none other than the lost Toltecs of Mexico. Joseph Jones suggested that perhaps the Toltecs and the Moon-Eyed People were related. If one looks at stone depictions of the Toltec, their eyes seem to be in a perpetual squint, which is also true of statues of the Moon-Eyed People.

Is it possible that these Moon-Eyed People were just human beings with abnormal genetic traits, or were they vampires? Unless stories of the blood drinking are true, it seems more likely that the Moon-Eyed People probably all shared a genetic trait that made them extremely sensitive to light.

---

[27] A vampiric entity called "Green Eyes" today haunts the nearby site of the Battle of Chickamauga.

⚔ COWBOYS & VAMPIRES ⚔

Vampire or not, if you want to see evidence of the Moon-Eyed People today, you can visit both the Cherokee County Historical Museum, where the effigies are contained, and also Fort Mountain State Park in Murray County, Georgia. Within the park is an ancient 885-foot-long rock wall that runs along the peak. The wall makes a zigzag pattern and also includes a stone gateway. It is said that the Moon-Eyed People built it, and a 1956 archaeological report stated that the structure "represents a prehistoric aboriginal construction whose precise age and nature cannot yet be safely hazarded until the whole problem, of which this is a representative, has been more fully investigated."

STONE FORMATION REMAINS IN FORT MOUNTAIN STATE PARK. [WIKIPEDIA]

CHAPTER 9

THE VARNER
VAMPIRE

At first glance, the following story might appear to be that of a typical wild-man running afoul of rural farmers. However, there are a few details that make this wild man something special. But first, the article itself, which comes from *The Dallas Morning News* of September 3, 1905:

> Nearly a year ago the people living along the river front near Preston [Texas] were set agog by the appearance in the woods of a strange being in human form. When discovered by a party of hunters on his all fours pawing and neighing like a horse, their attention was first attracted by what they took to be the whining of a startled horse in the undergrowth.

When advanced upon, the strange being ran off on his hands and feet but the pursuers gained upon him so rapidly he sprang to his feet and quickly covering the short distance to the river, plunged headlong from a rather high bank into the water and swam to the Indian side. When he reached that bank he stood up, shook himself like a horse just out of a bath, and with what might really be called a horse laugh ran off into the woods. Some months later he was seen under much the same conditions but this time west of Woodville, on the Indian side.

Only a few weeks ago a man crawled across the road in plain view of several people not far from where the horse-man was first seen but disappeared, the pursuit being somewhat tardy. Since Sunday last the people living near Colbert, ten miles east of Preston, Grayson County, Texas, have been hunting for a strangely acting man who crawled about like a snake until pursued, when he would jump to his feet and outrun the fastest horses ridden after him. Others who pursued him on foot say they shot at him at close range but the bullets, if they struck their target, seemed to have no effect.

As late as last evening, children claim to have seen the crawling man again near the Varner place, six miles from Colbert. A phone message from Colbert this afternoon confirms previous reports sent out from Durant about the state of excitement and the gathering of several parties for pursuit, but states that public interest has received something of a chill because some of the parties who were present when the close-range shots were fired say that although the peculiar being was in the open and very close, that he disappeared with the smoke of the powder.

At the Varner place he crawled into the henhouse. It is stated that out in the field a dead chicken, bitten in the neck, and from which there was the appearance of the blood having been drawn, was found.

Though with somewhat reduced enthusiasm, the people of the Varner neighborhood are preparing for another big roundup this afternoon and tonight.

Do I really think the man was a vampire? Probably not, but the "Varner Vampire" was irresistible as a title. That said, wouldn't a normal wild man have taken that chicken and eaten it rather than sucking its blood? And what about the wild man's reported imperviousness to bullets? Could have been attributed to hysteria or bad aim on the part of the hunters. Or, could it be that the wild man was possessed, hence his increased strength—a real attribute of possession—and animal-like behavior. In my book, that is the most likely conclusion.

MUMMY DISCOVERED IN NEVADA AWES AND PUZZLES SCIENTISTS

Object, Hideous in Aspect, Is Found on Mount Davidson,

SPECIAL DISPATCH TO THE CALL.

RENO, June 16.—What looks like a combination of Chinese devil and nightmare was brought to Carson today by J. B. Kenny and Ed. Wallis, who found the uncanny object high up on Mount Davidson yesterday. It is mummified and has a head like a human being, hair, nose, mouth and eyes, but it has no body. It is provided with wings like a bat and apparently, when alive, could do most anything from swimming in the water to sailing in the air like a kite. Professor Smith took a photograph of it and will send a copy to Professor Frandsen of the University of Nevada.

The head is about the size of a baseball and, though it has no body, it has legs like a frog. Sixty teeth, three of them broken, grace the mouth that perpetually grins, and everybody that looked at it was glad it was dead. It is absolutely a unique species of some animal that used to walk, swim or fly, according as its fancy chose.

CHAPTER 10
NEVADA'S VAMPIRE SKELETON

I t's odd when skeletal remains exhumed in the American Southwest can help corroborate a legend from the opposite side of the globe. If the story is true, that is... On June 21, 1906, *The Fort Worth Telegram* reported the following:

What looks like a combination of Chinese 'devil' and a nightmare was brought to Carson [Nevada] yesterday by J. R. Kenny and Ed Wallis who found the uncanny object high up on Mount Davidson [Storey County, Nevada].[28]

---

[28] Though I would love to say that Mount Davidson is the source of many legends, I could find none at all other than a UFO sighting at nearby Virginia City from back in the mid-1800s.

It is mummified and has a head like a human being; a pair of noses, mouth and eyes, but it has no body. It is provided with wings like a bat and apparently when alive could do most anything from swimming in water to sailing in the air like a kite. Professor Smith took a photograph of it and will send a copy to Professor Fransend of the University of Nevada. The head is about the size of a baseball and has legs like a frog. Six teeth, three of them broken, grace a mouth which perpetually grins. It is an absolutely unique species of some animal that used to walk, swim or fly, according as its fancy chose.

The "Chinese 'devil'" mentioned in passing at the article's beginning was likely a reference to vampiric flying heads, which are a common part of Asian folklore, particularly with the yokai of Japan. Most likely, they were referring to the Nukekubi, an otherwise normal-looking human being whose head could detach itself from its body. The disembodied heads then float through the night and terrify their prey by issuing a bloodcurdling scream, after which they will sink their teeth into them and feed.

Allegedly such a vampire existed in the capital city of Echizen, where the disembodied head of a young woman would chase young men. Supposedly the young woman was unaware of her affliction as she blacked out during the incidents, but when she learned, she committed suicide.

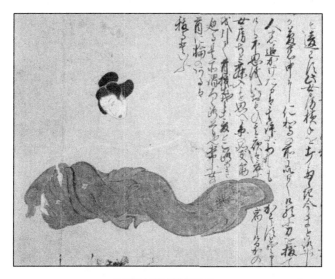

THE NUKEKUBI.

Closer to home, and to the skeleton itself, is a flying vampire head of Iroquois mythology.[29] In their case, the flying head has wings just like the skeleton unearthed on Mount Davidson. The Chonchon of South America is also a disembodied human head that can fly and suck the lifeblood of its victims. Such beings are created when kalku (Mapuche sorcerers) anoint themselves with a magical cream that allows the head to detach from the body. The ears of the Chonchon then become so large that they serve as wings so that the head can fly through the air.

---

[29] The Iroquois comprise of five tribes in the Northeastern U.S. including the Mohawk, Oneida, Onondaga, Cayuga, and Seneca.

One has to wonder if perhaps the writer of the article simply intended the whole thing as a hoax, as they were certainly aware of the myth of flying, disembodied heads from Asia. (They said nothing about similar myths from the Americas, so must have been unaware of them.) But what if the find was real and represented a strange, now-extinct animal that birthed the legends of flying heads the world over? The article does state that a photo of the head was sent to Professor Fransend of the University of Nevada.

While many skeptics will simply say that the absence of such a photograph today is "proof" that it never happened, skeptics never account for the fact that many institutions simply cover up finds that don't agree with their view of the world, much like allegations that the Smithsonian suppresses many of the giant skeletons found since time immemorial. And yes, Peter "Bugs" Frandsen, was a well-known Nevada biology professor at the university, though using a famous scientist in a hoax was nothing new in terms of yellow journalism.

CHAPTER 11
MEXICAN VAMPIRE TREE

arlier in this book we covered the mysterious vampire tree of Lafayette, Colorado, but as it turns out, Mexico has an even more unique vampire tree. In El Panteon de Belen Cemetery in Guadalajara, Mexico, is another such example.[30]

Just as in Lafayette, there's little to back up the claim that the tree in question relates to a vampire. So the story goes, "many years ago"[31] Guadalajara was plagued by a series of animal deaths wherein said animals were drained of blood. As this took

[30] Said cemetery has many legends aside from the vampire tree involving pirates, ghosts, and even one which relates to José Cuervo (the man, not the drink).
[31] Mexico Unexplained guesses that this was probably the mid-1800s.

place well before the Chupacabra craze of the 1990s, the deaths were attributed to a traditional vampire.

POSTCARD DEPICTING EL PANTEON DE BELEN.

Next, the vampire moved on to human infants, draining them of all blood in the night so that their horrified mothers found them dead the next morning. When the citizens of Guadalajara had finally had enough, some of them conducted a stake-out in the town late at night. They eventually spotted a curiously pale-skinned man with light-colored eyes skulking through the streets. (Could it have been a rare example of a male Tlahuelpuchi?)

Since another vampire attack had occurred that night, and the man looked so strange, the villagers followed him back to his home and killed him. (An alternate version of the story goes that several suspects were rounded up, and the palest man of the bunch was singled out as the vampire.) There was no trial conducted, the villagers simply felt that since the man was so strange looking, he must have been to blame and drove a stake through his heart.

THE "TREE OF THE VAMPIRE" IN EL PANTEON DE BELEN.

The villagers buried the vampire in Panteón de Belén under several slabs of concrete to hinder any efforts of the corpse to rise from the dead again. A few months later, villagers made the disturbing discovery that a tree had grown up through the concrete. Like the Lafayette Vampire, they said it sprouted from the stake in the vampire's chest. Whether the story of the vampire is true or not, there is a large tree there.

The legend of the "Tree of the Vampire" continues to grow, as it is said that the faces of the vampire's victims can sometimes be seen in the bark. It is also said that if one breaks off a branch from the tree, it will ooze blood rather than sap. City officials even placed a special fence around the tree to protect it, for if it were ever to die, it is said the vampire would rise again...

Sources:

Bitto, Robert. "The Legends of the Santa Paula Cemetery." Mexico Unexplained (March 13, 2017) https://mexicounexplained.com/legends-santa-paula-cemetery/

CHAPTER 12
LEGEND OF GREEN EYES

The Battle of Chickamauga was one of the bloodiest battles in the Civil War. It is ranked by many as second only to the Battle of Gettysburg in terms of how many people died. The Battle of Chickamauga raged for two days (September 19–20) in 1863 in southeastern Tennessee and northwestern Georgia.

Legend has it that the battle was preceded by a bad omen. The night before the fight began, two Tennessee soldiers supposedly heard an unearthly shriek come from the woods. The soldiers crept to the edge of the foliage and glimpsed a hairy, ten-foot-tall monster. Its eyes glowed like hot coals, and it smelt like rotten meat. When the soldiers ran back to camp to tell their commander of what they saw, no one believed them. The next morning, a sergeant went to the spot where they saw the creature and found 22-inch footprints in the earth of the Sasquatch variety.

But Bigfoot wasn't the only strange creature associated with the battle. A strange being today called "Green Eyes" was also glimpsed. The human-like creature was seen after the battle was over, and witnesses claimed that it was feeding on the bodies of the dead! It was humanoid in form but with great jaws full of fanged teeth. It was said to be short and had long straw-like hair flowing from its head. It also had glowing green eyes that struck terror into those who saw them.

THE BATTLE OF CHICKAMAUGA.

Some legends later claimed that it was the ghost of a soldier killed during the battle. What's more, it's still seen at the site of the Battle of Chickamauga to this day.

GREEN EYES BY NEIL RIEBE.

There have been a few stories about the drivers of cars seeing the intense, glowing green eyes when they drive near the battlefield. A few times, the eyes were so intense that they caused the driver to have an accident. Two wrecks that people know of occurred in the 1970s.

> Unfortunately, the locale of this story is unknown, as names like the "Battle Ground" are common among multiple states. However, if the blurb isn't referring to Green Eyes, then it's certainly another entity just like it. In any case, the article was published in the *Delphi Weekly Times* on June 22, 1883:
>
> —The Lafayette Cornier chronicles the depredations of a strange shining black monster, with red hair and gleaming eyes, resembling, in an outlandish sort of way, a woman, that has been terrifying people living near Battle Ground. The monster may be there...

In 1976, a park ranger named Edward Tinney said that he was walking through the park at 4 A.M. when he saw Green Eyes. He said that before it appeared, a chill coursed through his body. And then he saw it: a green-eyed being stepping from the shadows.

"When it passed me, I could see his hair was long like a woman's," Tinney said. "The eyes – I'll never forget those eyes – they were glaring, almost greenish-orange in color, flashing like some sort of wild animal. The teeth were long and pointed like fangs."

The monster mysteriously disappeared when the headlights of a car driving by illuminated it. Be it a ghoul or a ghostly vampire, if you like to tour old battlegrounds of the Civil War, beware of Chickamauga...

CHAPTER 13
VAMPIRE MEDICINE MAN

Vampires can come in all shapes and sizes—even miniature. Cultures the world over have tales of mischievous Little People who often live underground and abduct surface dwellers. And sometimes they drink blood. Enter the mysterious "Little People" of Native American legend. They went by a different name in each tribe, and rumors of vampiric Little People dated back to the conquistadors. Hernando de Soto heard tales of cave-dwelling beings that drank blood to the north in what is today Wyoming. Even Lewis and Clark were told of vicious, subterranean dwarves who lived in mounds and supposedly drank blood and ate human flesh.

And where do these magical beings come from? According to Mesoamerican myth and legend, the earth has been created, destroyed, and recreated several times over, a belief also shared by many Native Americans. According to some, these blood-drinking imps were survivors of one of the previous worlds. Their size varied from being gigantic in stature to normal-sized to tiny imps, which were the most common. Like the Moon-Eyed People, sometimes these beings were said to only come out at night, specifically to hunt. An alternate legend, this one more vampiric in nature, stated that these beings used to be men but had transformed into a new life form.

Most pertinent to this chapter are the Little People as portrayed by the Crow nation, who alternately called them the Nirumbee or the Awwakkule. Like vampires, they claimed that these people were more or less ancient and possibly immortal. As such, they were to be feared and respected. To cross one of the Nirumbee was to die, but to get on their good side and seek their advice was very favorable. The main reason that these people were sometimes associated with vampires was that they used blood in their rituals. (This actually isn't uncommon the world over, just look at the Aztecs.)

The chief of the Crow Nation, Plenty Coups, was said to have had several visions and dreams from the Little People, beginning at age nine, that significantly shaped his future leadership of the tribe. The spiritual insight received from the Little People led directly to the Crow Nation remaining strong even after most of the other tribes were broken and scattered across North America.

PLENTY COUPS.

The visions influenced Plenty Coups to promote education for his people and to try to keep alive the culture and beliefs of the Crow well into the future, while other tribes lost so much of their cultural identities. In one of the most influential of these visions, the Chief of the Little People revealed to Plenty Cous that the white men would swarm over the land but that if he took certain steps, his tribe would survive into the future.

His first encounter with the magic shaman occurred when he was nine years old during his initiation ceremony as a warrior. On a vision quest, the chief of the Little People appeared before him and showed Plenty Coups the future. He explained something of his people's history, too, stating that they were an ancient race that had lived on the Great Plains long before the Crow or any other tribes arrived. He also let slip the ominous detail that he and his people were blood drinkers and that to summon them, blood needed to be spilled. Two years later, at age 11, on another vision quest, Plenty Coups waited several days for the little medicine man to appear again, only he didn't. Remembering his words from last time, Plenty Coups cut into his index finger, letting the blood flow. At that point, the little chief returned. Something of a shapeshifter, which is not uncommon in vampiric beings, the little chief transformed into an old man with a buffalo-like face this time. He led him through a system of underground tunnels within the Pryor Mountains filled with buffalo. Soon after, he warned of the coming invasion of the white men. The vision showed that "the day of the Plains Indian was ending, and that white men would swarm over the land like buffalo. But the chickadee [a very small bird representing the Crow Nation] remains, because it is a good listener, develops its mind, and survives by its wits." Today, the spot where Plenty Coups allegedly emerged from under the ground is now known as Chief Plenty Coups State Park in Montana.

In addition to their incredible strength, the Little People practiced "powerful medicine," according to the Crow. In one story, a young Crow boy accidentally fell into a bonfire, leaving his face horribly scarred. He was given the name "Burnt Face" after the accident. Time passed, and the boy decided to summon the Little People, which he did by spilling blood to the ground. Soon he was met by several of the dwarves. After talking with the boy, the Little People tended to his scars, causing them to completely disappear. They also gave him healing powers to help his people. When Burnt Face returned to his people, he retained his name, but his newfound skills enabled him to become a great chief among his people.

In stark contrast to Plenty Coups and the Crow, the Arapaho were sworn enemies with the Little People, who they called Hecesiiteihii or Nimerigar. For instance, these Little People were said to trap the souls of warriors in jars for eternity via their magical powers. Like vampires, these Little People were very hard to kill, and arrows seemed to have little effect on them. A war was fought with these Little People, who were eventually trapped within a gorge and killed. Like vampires, the Arapaho held a belief that these beings could not cross running water, and so to escape them, all one needed to do was jump or swim across a river.

Likewise, the Cheyenne and Shoshone stated that these people abhorred sunlight in addition to sharing a kinship with the dead. The Nez Perce Native American tribe alleged that the beings could turn themselves invisible with a special grass. The Shoshone considered the Little People to be tricksters, and blamed most of their bad luck on them. Similar to the Nimerigar was another tribe called the Nirumbee, which would sometimes abduct children. And, when it suited them, they drank blood. Specifically, they liked to kill the elderly when they were of no further use and drink their blood, believing that they absorbed their many years of wisdom in the process.

MUMMIFIED PYGMY FOUND

LUSK, Wyo.—(U.P.)—A mummified pygmy, believed by scientists to be a progenitor of the present human race, was exhibited in Lusk recently. The mummy is owned by Homer F. Sherrill, of Crawford, Neb., and has baffled scientists in various parts of the country where it has been sent for classification. It was unearthed in a cave on a slope of one of the Peaks of Pedro mountain, near Casper, Wyo.

Though tales of the Little People may sound like pure folklore, what may be proof of their existence was discovered in 1932 in the San Pedro Mountains of Wyoming. In July of 1934, Cecil Main and Frank Carr were mining for gold there. While tracing a seam of gold into the rock face of the mountain, they ran into a dead end. They had no choice but to blast into the rock face. To their disappointment, when the smoke cleared, they found no more gold. However, the explosion revealed a hidden cave within the mountain.

THE SAN PEDRO MUMMY

The cave measured four feet wide and fifteen feet long. Sitting cross-legged on a ledge was a tiny mummy only six inches tall. It had been mummified from the natural elements over time, and as such most of its features were still intact and discernable. And what strange features they were. A strange, black, jelly-like substance covered the head, and the facial features were odd, with a low, flat forehead and flattened nose. Then there were the rather bulbous eyes and the full set of teeth—I point out the teeth because if the tiny six-inch mummy was a fetus, as some argue, then it shouldn't have had teeth.

Little Pedro would seem to have died a violent death unbefitting of a little baby, as his skull appeared to have been smashed along with a broken collarbone and a damaged spine. Remember accounts of the Little People bashing in the heads of the elderly to kill them?

You may now be asking why proper testing hasn't been conducted on Pedro recently. That's because, unfortunately, Pedro mysteriously disappeared in the 1950s. Until he is rediscovered, his true nature will remain a mystery.

Sources:

Curran, Dr. Bob and Ian Daniels. *American Vampires: Their True Bloody History From New York to California.* Weiser (October 22, 2012)

CHAPTER 14
VAMPIRE CHAIR OF TENNESSEE

The following tale begins very appropriately with the discovery of a dead body buried at a crossroads. And not just any random dead body. It was buried facedown, had been partially mummified from minerals in the ground, and most important of all, it had a stake driven through its heart.

The year was 1917 and the body was found near Oostanaula Creek in Bradley County, Tennessee, not far from Charleston. It was discovered by a road crew working to widen a road that curved around a river bluff. Those familiar with legends of the Crossroads Demon will no doubt find it interesting that the body was discovered at a crossroads itself. As stated before, it was petrified, and this being the year 1917, that meant it had been buried at some point the previous century.

As the workers examined the body, they discovered the wooden stake through the heart. Nor was it a stake carved for that purpose. Ever seen a vampire movie where the hero grabs a fencepost or a broken chair leg to impale the vampire? That's apparently what happened here, as the men were able to determine that it was indeed a chair leg and not a petrified piece of wood.

They were able to tell because it wasn't just any old chair leg, but a very ornate one that must've come from a wealthy home. Back then, chairs were a big deal, as they signified one's financial well-standing depending on how nice they were. The workmen recognized the chair leg as the work of Eli and Jacob Odom, a couple of early-day Tennessee settlers renowned for their distinctive chair designs, notably the "mule-eared chair."

Local lore referred to the corpse as "the woman from Hiwassee" and "the witch lady". Some think that her name was remembered but locals were too fearful to utter it out loud. This wasn't unique to Tennessee, and many cultures attribute a certain power or taboo to speaking a powerful name aloud. Native Americans don't like to utter the names of witches or skinwalkers as they fear that it will draw them near. So, that the Appalachian peoples were fearful of uttering the alleged witch's name wasn't out of left field.

Oral tradition says that in life the witch woman had the stereotypical appearance of a witch as an old hag with dry skin reminiscent of a snake and mouth that emitted foul breath. Naturally, she lived in a lonely cabin on the bluff and rarely ventured out unless she had to buy supplies. Animals seemed to fear her, and birds shied away from her cabin. The people of the area shunned her publicly but were said to visit her in secret when her services were desired.

She used local plant life to create powerful potions to either cure ailments or induce them. She could also make love potions and she was said to have attributes of what we would call the skinwalker in the Southwest, being able to transform into a bird, specifically a crow.

Of course, witches were usually burned at the stake or drowned, so why the stake in the heart? That's because, allegedly, she also drank blood. (It apparently didn't do her haggard appearance any favors.) The locals whispered that she would sneak into men's homes as they slept and feed on them. Some said she gained ingress into the house in the form of a black rat, and in that form, she would feed on small children. Others even claimed they had seen her transform into a big black bird on her way to and from victims' homes. However, some have theorized that the woman probably never actually sank her fangs into anyone's neck, and in truth, she used blood in her rituals and potions, and from that the vampire aspect of the story took root.

It is said that the vampire witch's end came about due to an epidemic sweeping the area. Back in those days, vampires and witches were often associated with plagues and illnesses. When a particularly virulent one hit the Charleston area sometime in the early to mid-1800s, it is said that area residents began to blame the old witch up on the bluff. The perennial angry mob of the old Universal monster movies then descended on the witch's cabin and dragged her from it to her death.

In the book, *The Granny Curse and Other Ghosts and Legends from East Tennessee,* an old quote from the *Tennessee Folklore Society Bulletin* pertaining to the land the witch supposedly lived on was reprinted. The land had been owned by the family of the now deceased Frank G. Trewhitt, who stated, "The land on which the body was found belonged to my great-grandfather and was passed to his sons. If they ever had heard any vampire tales hereabouts, I would have been told."

For those wondering if there might be some other, more logical explanation for a woman found buried at a crossroads with a stake through her heart, there really are none. Let's say a woman did suffer a freak accident where she had a chair leg impaled in her chest, it's unlikely she would have been buried in the middle of nowhere. (Unless, perhaps, she was murdered for some reason.)

Wooden stakes aside, it's also important to note that the woman was buried facedown. In the "Old Country" (i.e. Eastern Europe) burying a vampire facedown was a common custom and served as a way of ensuring that it didn't dig its way back to the surface, the thought process being that when it began to claw its way through the dirt, it would dig itself deeper and deeper into the earth. They were also buried at crossroads because it was thought that if they emerged, the intersection may confuse them and they would not know which way to go. Plus, the frequent passing of horses and wagons would keep the ground packed firmly in place. Anyhow, while we can't prove that the corpse found along the crossroads in 1917 really was a vampire, it's certainly obvious that whoever killed the woman believed she was.

ORNATE ANTIQUE CHAIR.

But the story still doesn't end there. Believe it or not, a legend is also attached to the chair that the leg was broken off of to impale the witch! And, actually, this legend might just be more interesting than the story of the witch itself.

According to lore, and in spite of what you might expect, the villagers didn't burn the witch's abode down after they were done with her. Sensible folk, they instead ransacked the house and divided her more valuable belongings amongst themselves, including the Odom chair with the leg broken off. The chair was repaired and taken to someone's residence. But, the occupants soon noticed that the chair itself had become a vampire! That's right, a vampire chair. Supposedly, the chair felt comfortable at first until suddenly, inexplicably, the sitter suddenly feels stuck to the chair, as if they are being drained of their energy and cannot stand. Eventually, a scratch would appear on either the forearm or the leg, and a small drop of blood would fall to the floor under the chair. After that, the occupant could finally stand and escaped the cursed chair.

Naturally, someone eventually got the idea to destroy the chair, but how does one stake a piece of vampire furniture made of wood? Supposedly, when residents went to destroy it, it was supernaturally impervious to their blows and so they gave it away. Other stories said that residents were actually too frightened to destroy the chair and never even tried for fear of another curse falling upon them, and so they simply set it in an abandoned area for some other poor soul to come along and collect it.

The chair made the rounds and was allegedly last seen at various locations across Tennessee, either on the porch a hotel near Charleston, an old house in Greeneville, at an antiques shop in Kingsport and so on. Others whisper it has traveled out of state, and maybe even out of the country to Europe, where the old witch woman's spirit still haunts it. But, just in case the Europe story isn't true, be wary of antique chairs in Tennessee...

Sources:

Curran, Dr. Bob and Ian Daniels. *American Vampires: Their True Bloody History From New York to California.* Weiser (October 22, 2012)

Russel, Randy and Janet Barnett. *The Granny Curse and Other Ghosts and Legends from East Tennessee.* Blair, 1999.

NOSFERATU, RELEASED IN 1922, THREE
YEARS BEFORE THE CHURCH HILL
TUNNEL COLLAPSE.

CHAPTER 15
THE RICHMOND VAMPIRE

On October 2, 1925, a railroad tunnel collapsed in Church Hill, Virginia, killing four men and burying a locomotive along with ten cars. The tunnel had been built back in 1873 and was already out of commission by 1901. In 1925, it was decided to restore the tunnel, and that's when the collapse happened. About 200 workers managed to survive by crawling under the train cars until they reached the east end of the tunnel and managed to get back to the outside world. As stated before, the final death tally amounted to four men as far as authorities could tell. Rescue efforts only resulted in further collapses, and so the tunnel was sealed off for safety reasons. According to urban legend, one man emerged from the rubble with blood dripping from his mouth and torn flesh hanging from his limbs. This account, true or not, was later conjoined with another area legend called the Richmond Vampire.

UNDATED IMAGE OF EAST TUNNEL OF CHURCH HILL AFTER COLLAPSE.

Much like the other vampires covered in this book, the Richmond Vampire had that moniker bestowed upon him after his death, which occurred in 1922, by the way, three years before the tunnel collapse. Buried in the Hollywood Cemetery[32] of Richmond, Virginia, the deceased's name was W.W. Pool, and supposedly the vampire rumor began simply because the W's reminded people of fangs! It didn't hurt that the Pool's tomb had design aesthetics of the Egyptian Rite of Freemasonry, which only added to the mystique.

---

[32] Jefferson Davis and James Monroe are also buried there.

In the 1960s, a story came about that Pool was from England and had been run out of his own country for being a vampire. Specifically, it is thought that students cooked up the story at the nearby Virginia Commonwealth University, and by 1976 the tale was published in the *Commonwealth Times*.

**THE VAMPIRE'S TOMB
IN HOLLYWOOD CEMETERY.**
[RVA ALL DAY CC BY-SA 4.0]

According to the article by Garry F. Curtis,

Mr. Pool is an alleged vampire. There seems to be a cult in Richmond that has grown up around him. I find this strange since I've heard that it used to be the 'in' thing among medical students to break in and steal parts of his remains. My informant also claims that W.W. was the inspiration for Barnabas Collins on the old

Gothic soap opera 'Dark Shadows.' I take this bit of news with a grain of salt, however.

In the mid-1980s, occultists took notice of the legend and began using the mausoleum as a backdrop for their rituals. According to Harry Kollatz Jr. in an article in *Richmond Magazine*, "the iron door of his crypt got jimmied open and fanciful occultists inscribed words and symbols on the outer chamber's walls. Fetishes are still dropped by the gate with some regularity. The glass of the lunette window on the inner wall shattered (presumably from the inside)."[33]

In the early 21st Century, someone decided to combine the Richmond Vampire with the Churchill Tunnel collapse. The new story claimed that the blood-drenched, muscular man seen emerging from the tunnel had been feeding on one of the dead. Furthermore, it was the tunnel collapse itself that had somehow awakened this ancient evil. Men chased the ghoulish creature all the way to James River and then into Hollywood Cemetery, where it took refuge in the crypt of W.W. Pool. Some say that as the men rushed into the crypt, the lid of the coffin was closing, while others say the vampire locked itself inside the mausoleum and no one could actually gain ingress.

Is there any truth to the tale of a badly wounded man emerging from the debris? Possibly. Gregory Maitland of the Virginia Ghosts & Haunting

---

[33] Kollatz Jr., "W.W. Pool: Richmond's Reputed Nosferatu", *Richmond Magazine*.

Research Society thinks the wounded man was the muscular Benjamin F. Mosby, who had been shoveling coal into the firebox of the steam locomotive in the tunnel when the collapse occurred. As a result, the boiler ruptured and he was badly burned. It is also said that his teeth were broken during the incident, making them jagged. Poor Mosby didn't live long after he emerged from the tunnel and was later buried in Hollywood Cemetery. That is a logical explanation, as Mosby was, for a fact, a real man who died after emerging badly injured from the tunnel. He also had all the physical characteristics of the alleged vampire, including the muscular physique.

Neither was Poole found to be an English vampire on the run, by the way, and was simply a local accountant for the wealthy Bryan family, owners of the *Richmond Times-Dispatch.* It is thought that he was being frugal when he had his initials placed on the tomb rather than his full name, and the double W's were later interpreted as fangs by excitable college students. As such, the so-called Hollywood Vampire is just as fictitious as anything that ever came out of Tinseltown.

Sources:

Kollatz Jr., Harry. "W.W. Pool: Richmond's Reputed Nosferatu", *Richmond Magazine* (October 30, 2013). https://richmondmagazine.com/arts-entertainment/richmonds-reputed-nosferatu/

⟨ COWBOYS & VAMPIRES ⟩

ANOTHER VIRGINIA VAMPIRE

A decade before the more famous Richmond Vampire incident is this tale from 1909. The story appeared in the *Baltimore Sun* on March 28, 1909, on page 11:

NEGRO A VAMPIRE Murderer Gorged Himself On Blood Of Hogs.
ALWAYS FOLLOWED BUTCHER
One Of Men Who Killed Mrs. Skipwith And Burned Southeast Was like An Animal.

[Special Dispatch to the Baltimore Sun.]
Richmond, Va., March 27.—John and William Brown, father and son, condemned in Powhatan county for the electric chair April 30 for the murder of Mrs. Mary E. Skipwith and Walter G. Johnson in that county, and the burning of Mrs. Skipwith's home, Southeast, in which the bodies, that of the man still alive, were cremated, were brought to the Henrico county jail this morning, where they will remain until taken to the State penitentiary for execution.

A remarkable fact stated this morning by William Simpson, a farmer living near the Skipwith plantation, on which Brown had lived all his days, shown that all his life Brown has been a man of the most beastly and repulsive appetite, absolutely without feeling or kindness, and without the slightest conception of affection.

"Whenever Brown heard there were to be hog killings in the neighborhood of his home," said Simpson, "he would make it his business to go to that place and be there when the hogs were killed. As a hog, with its throat cut, would stagger from the hands of the butcher, Brown would push upon it and, holding the animal with both hands, apply his mouth to the wound and drink the blood of the hog. The warm blood of the animal seemed to have the same effect on Brown that the taste of human blood had on the vampire. When he had gorged himself to repletion he appeared intoxicated and sodden to the extent that he could scarcely move around."

Simpson, who is a reputable farmer, states that a man saw Brown drink at least a half gallon of the blood of a hog in a morning, and had seen him do the thing a dozen times. It appears to be a well-known fact in the vicinity in which Brown lived that he was a human vampire. In appearance Brown is not an unusual negro, although it is stated that his brain planned the conspiracy to murder and burn the Skipwith home and to commit other depredations throughout the countryside.

The other prisoners, Joe and Isham Taylor und Lewis Jenkins, will go to the electric chair on April 30.

REMOVED TO U. S. ASYLUM.

He was Charged With Being a Vampire and Living on Human Blood.

[By Associated Press to the NEWS.]

COLUMBUS, Ohio, Nov. 4.—Deputy U. S. Marshall Williams, of Cincinnati, has removed James Brown, a deranged U. S. prisoner, from the Ohio penitentiary to the National Asylum, Washington, D. C. The prisoner fought them like a tiger against being removed. Twenty-five years ago he was charged with being a vampire and living on human blood.

He was a Portuguese sailor and shipped on a fishing smack from Boston up the coast in 1867. During the trip two of the crew were missing and an investigation was made. Brown was found one day in the hold of the ship sucking the blood from the body of one of the sailors. The other body was found at the same place and had been served in a similar manner.

Brown was returned to Boston and convicted of murder and sentenced to be hanged. President Johnson commuted the sentence to imprisonment for life. After serving 15 years in Massachusetts, he was transferred to the Ohio prison. He has committed two murders since his confinement. When being taken from the prison he believed that he was on his way to execution, and resisted accordingly.

CHAPTER 16
PRESIDENTIAL PARDON FOR A VAMPIRE

In the first chapter, we covered the 1892 vampire case out of Exeter that helped influence *Dracula*. That same year, another story ran in the papers describing a human vampire. In this case, it even greatly resembled a scene from *Dracula*. In the novel, Dracula boards the ship *Demeter* and on the voyage stalks and kills the crew. The article told of a mental patient who had been locked up many years ago for attacking his fellow crewmen on a seagoing vessel and drinking their blood! As for another odd coincidence, the man's name was Brown, the same as the alleged vampire from Exeter in 1892.

COWBOYS & VAMPIRES

The story was published in the *Brooklyn Daily Eagle* on November 4, 1892, on page one:

A HUMAN VAMPIRE AND A MURDERER

THE TERRIBLE RECORD OF A MANIAC CONVICT - REMOVED TO AN ASYLUM.

COLUMBUS, OH., November 4 - Deputy United States Marshal Williams of Cincinnati has removed James Brown, a deranged United States prisoner, from the Ohio penitentiary to the national asylum in Washington D.C. The prisoner fought like a tiger against being removed.

25 years ago he was charged with being a vampire and living on human blood. He was a Portuguese sailor and shipped on a fishing smack from Boston up the coast in 1867. During the trip two of the crew were missing and an investigation made. Brown was found one day in the hold of the ship sucking the blood from the body of one of the sailors. The other body was found at the same place and had been served in a similar manner. Brown was returned to Boston and convicted of murder and sentenced to be hanged. President Johnson commuted the sentence to imprisonment for life.

After serving 15 years in Massachusetts he was transferred to the Ohio prison. He has committed to murder since his confinement.

When being taken from the prison he believed that he was on his way to execution and resisted accordingly.

However, this article didn't cause near the stir that the Mercy Brown story did. As stated before, Stoker for certain read the Mercy Brown story in the *New York World* because a newspaper clipping of it was found in Stoker's papers. However, I wouldn't be surprised if Stoker read this article as well, all things considered.

Since then, many researchers have dug a little deeper into the strange case of James Brown, notably Robert Schneck, author of *The President's Vampire*.[34] Schneck and others were able to clarify that James "Jimmy" Brown was 25 years old when he perpetrated the attacks on board the *Atlantic* in May of 1866. He was said to be small, dark-skinned, heavily tattooed, and had reportedly been born in Georgetown, Guyana, in 1839. He was working as a cook in New Bedford when he got the job on the *Atlantic*.[35] He was notorious for his bad temper and routinely fought and quarreled with his fellow sailors on the long voyages.

Though the article I reprinted from 1892 was vague in terms of how he murdered his fellow crewmen—and one might be forgiven for thinking he bit them on the neck—the real story is a bit more

---

[34] A well-done collection of odd historical stories of which Brown's got the title nod.

[35] It's worth noting that the *Atlantic*, just like the fictitious *Demeter* from *Dracula*, also ran aground in 1887 off the coast of San Francisco, killing 27 of the 38 crew.

mundane. Brown's victim was 19-year-old James Foster, who insulted Brown with some form of racial slur in the kitchen. It is said that Brown stabbed Foster with a six-inch double-edged sheath knife on the left side of his chest to a depth of four inches. Within minutes Foster bled out and died. The incident was witnessed by James W. Gardner, who reported it to Captain Benjamin Franklin Wing. According to the *Atlantic*'s own logbook, Wing had Brown shackled in double-irons within the brig. Brown and Gardner, to serve as witness, were transferred to another ship as soon as possible to go to Boston for trial. There was no mention in the logbook of Brown drinking blood.

PRESIDENT ANDREW JOHNSON.

The first account to allege that Brown perpetrated a vampiric act came about nearly twenty years later in the *Boston Globe* on June 26, 1885, which alleged that Brown, "...in 1865 killed his captain at sea and drank his blood from the cloven skull."

Though Brown was initially sentenced to hang, for some reason he managed to get a pardon from President Andrew Johnson on January 3, 1867, on the basis that Brown appeared to be insane. (It wasn't just Brown, by the way, Johnson issued more pardons than any president in history.) Instead of being executed, Brown would spend the rest of his days in prison instead.

CHARLESTOWN STATE PRISON C.1833.

At first, he was sent to the Charlestown State Prison, notorious for being a bleak and abusive institution. In 1873, Brown struck again with another stabbing when he killed a fellow inmate.

He stabbed him seven times and the incident sent Brown into isolation for the next 12 years. According to the June 26, 1885 *Boston Globe* article, "He raged in his cell like a tiger in a cage." He was formally declared insane in June of 1885, hence the article that appeared in the *Boston Globe*. There were reasons other than the stabbing that Brown was considered insane. He was incredibly paranoid about anyone ever trying to enter his cell, and in particular he guarded an old Latin book in which he stored precious documents, including his pardon from President Johnson. Supposedly, when agitated, Brown's eyes would "shine out like coals of fire."[36]

ST. ELIZABETH'S MENTAL HOSPITAL.

He was transferred to St. Elizabeth's Mental Hospital in Washington, D.C. Only two years later

[36] "The Case of the Vampire who Wasn't", Providentia.
drvitelli.typepad.com/providentia/2019/06/was-james-brown-a-vampire.html

in 1887, Brown was declared to not in fact be insane, and was transferred to the Ohio State Penitentiary. By this time he was supposedly more docile due to being 50 years old and suffering from cataracts. By 1889, he was allowed to work outside every so often. That all ended when he stabbed a guard with his fork one day. He began to go back into crazy territory again when he began making claims that he was a rich railroad magnate among other things. He also let his fingernails grow so long that they came to resemble talons.

In 1892 came the move back to St. Elizabeth's. Since the move occurred in 1892, some think that a reporter latched onto the fact that his name was Brown like the Exeter vampires and decided to expound upon rumors that this Brown, too, was a bloodsucker. Another 1892 article alleged that before being brought back to St. Elizabeth's, Brown "killed one of his keepers with a chair, and when discovered he was lapping his victim's blood."[37]

According to a 1904 inquiry on behalf of the Charleston Prison, James Brown died on December 15, 1895, and was buried in the hospital cemetery. The 1895 date is intriguing for the fact that the vampiric incidents of the midwest also occurred earlier that year. You may recall that one of those cases involved a vampire inmate escaping an asylum and killing a man in Sioux City, Iowa. I

---

[37] Brumfield, "An American Nosferatu," Medium.
https://medium.com/lessons-from-history/an-american-nosferatu-dc13b2f6ce80

wondered if perhaps it was Brown for a time, but apparently not.

Again, considering that the ship's log says nothing of Brown drinking blood, we can only assume his vampiric characteristics can be attributed to a thirsty reporter rather than a thirsty vampire.

Sources:

Brumfield, Dale M. "An American Nosferatu." Lessons from History. (April 1, 2019) https://medium.com/lessons-from-history/an-american-nosferatu-dc13b2f6ce80

Schneck, Robert Damon. *The President's Vampire Strange -but-True Tales of The United States of America.* Barnes & Noble, 2007.

"The Case of the Vampire who Wasn't." Providentia (June 16, 2019) https://drvitelli.typepad.com/providentia/2019/06/was-james-brown-a-vampire.html

CHAPTER 17
INTERVIEW WITH THE VAMPIRE'S VICTIM

You've no doubt heard of Anne Rice's now classic vampire novel *Interview with the Vampire*, but back in the spring of 1897, papers across the country published an interview with the purported victim of a vampire. This particular reproduction comes from the April 21, 1897, *Anaconda Standard.*

HAUNTED BY A VAMPIRE.
California Railroad Man Who Is Pursued by a Relentless Enemy.

Alameda Letter to San Francisco Chronicle.

COWBOYS & VAMPIRES

John Santine, a well-known brake-man employed on the local narrow-gauge system, formerly for many years under Conductor Robert Owen on the Alameda broad-gauge line, says that he is the victim of a most extraordinary, relentless and supernatural enemy, which robs him of rest at night, and for several years has made his life a horrid nightmare.

"For about three years and a half I have been fighting ghosts at my house, 2544 Clement Avenue," said he to-day.

"A mysterious, uncanny intruder has kept me in a constant state of nervousness at night when I wanted to sleep. I thought for a long time it might be some 'varmint,' and set all sorts of pitfalls and snares to catch it. I had my bedroom, where I sleep alone, just filled with traps—mousetraps, rat-traps, 'figure 4s,' and deadfalls big enough to kill an alligator, but nothing ever came of it.

"As these singular nocturnal disturbances continued I came to the conclusion finally that I must be afflicted with a ghost. I bought a pistol and increased my watchfulness. At the least noise I would jump up and grab my pistol, but I never saw anything in the room.

"The curious thing about the affair was that after each disturbance, usually some time about the middle of the night, I would wake up to find myself covered with strange insects that died when exposed to the light. I bought all kinds of insect powder to beat the deuce—you just ask the druggist—but it didn't do any good. Then I

144

tried putting two cats in the room, but not a rat or mouse could be discovered.

"I feel sure now that the creature is a vampire, which comes to my bed and lays itself on my neck, for what purpose I cannot tell.

"It was only last Monday morning, about 2 o'clock, that I awoke suddenly and felt an object resting on my left shoulder. In a twinkling it flitted away. I heard it pattering along the pillow as it went, and I am certain it was the creature, vampire or what you will, that has been haunting me so long. It always has the most horrid smell, just like something from the grave, and I think it the odor as much as anything which wakes me up.

"I have always left my window open at the top to have plenty of air, but it never occurred to me that the cause of my continual annoyance might find ingress in that way. Those vampires are awfully cunning creatures, and as soon as they see the least movement they are off like a flash. Sometimes the thing wouldn't come near for a week, so that though I tried to be on the watch all the time I could never catch it. I have fixed up a lot of snares, which hang across my room, and I hope to get it so tangled in them some night that I can shut the window before it escapes.

"I have awakened in the morning many a time with a sickness at the stomach, and I believe that it was that vampire's presence during the night that caused it. There are lots of cases of children that pine away under the care of a physician, and

I believe that night visits from these hideous creatures are responsible for it. I don't know whether my case is an isolated one or not, but I think people should know about it and take necessary precautions."

"Do you drink, Mr. Santine?" he was asked.

"Not a drop."

So, what are we to make of this strange story? For starters, it's odd that Mr. Santine never once actually complains of blood loss. If anything, the entity, whatever it was, seemed mostly to interfere with his sleep patterns. It would also appear as though the man believed that the "vampire" was visiting him in the form of a bat or other small animal, as he never implies the presence of a human being, only vermin and insects.

VINTAGE VAMPIRE BAT ENGRAVING BY GEORGE BERNARD

Though I have unfortunately misplaced the source, I have another, similar article about a Hungarian man—emigrated to America—who believed he was being plagued by a vampire, which came from the *Xenia Gazette*.

A physician of local fame in an Eastern city said to the writer recently "This is an age of queer mental and bodily delusions, despite its enlightenment. One of the oddest cases that I ever saw I was called on to treat the other day. A man came in to complain that his ankles were wounded. I found that the wounds were scratches, and expressed my surprise that he should have consulted a physician about a trifle. He said he often found the skin of his ankles broken in the same way on rising from bed. I suggested that he smooth the foot board, and not kick it so much. Then the real object of his visit came out. What do you think it was? With bated breath he whispered that he was the victim of a vampire, not a vampire bat, but a human vampire. Actually here was a sound, healthy, intelligent man cowering from the effects of that old superstition. He hinted to me that he knew who the vampire was, a former enemy; now deceased. He had come to me for a charm, or something, to exorcise his terrible visitor. I tried to laugh and chaff him out of the idea. Whether I succeeded I do not know."

The bit about the insects is also intriguing. Try as I might, I can find no lore wherein insects are left behind by a vampire, though I did find a few where a vampire might turn into an insect. The man's claim that the insects would die when they were exposed to light is also quite strange. I could find no type of bug that died upon exposure to light, either.

As it stands, the main supernatural aspect to this case is the smell, which shouldn't be ignored as supernatural entities do indeed stink, often of sulfur, though Mr. Santine likened the smell as to something dead. Lastly, try as I might, I could find no records of John Santine, and I'm sure his obituary could have proven to be quite interesting. If nothing else, that a man in 1897 could think he was being plagued by a vampire in California shows how widespread the belief in vampires could be.

CHAPTER 18
GREAT LAKES VAMPIRE PICTOGRAPH

There is a strange subset of vampire mythology pertaining to mischievous Little People which were also vampires as covered in a previous chapter. The Great Lakes region has various pictographs and cave drawings attributed to these magical Little People. One of them is rather sinister.

It was found by a prospector in the early 1900s in Ontonagon County, Michigan. The man, Lewis Calhoun, was hunting a copper vein in the Porcupine Mountains when he trekked down into a narrow gorge. He found no copper there, but in the gully's deepest depths, he found some very strange drawings. These pictographs depicted strange, hairy-faced men in canoes rowing across one of the Great Lakes. Nothing strange there apart from their appearance. It was the next pictograph that gave Calhoun the chills. In that depiction, the little men appeared to be gathered around a fallen member of their tribe and were drinking his blood.

POSTCARD OF PORCUPINE MOUNTAINS.

All the while, Calhoun had the strange feeling that he was being watched, and decided to begin making his way out of the rocky ravine. On the way out, he spotted something on the ground that looked to be a sharp, vampire-like tooth. Though later Calhoun speculated it could have just been a sharpened stone that resembled a tooth, he was spooked enough by the object that he didn't take it with him. All he knew was that his instincts told him that he had to get out of the canyon fast, and so he did.

Later, he returned with a party of miners and educated men to show them the strange pictographs. However, upon approaching the canyon, it was clear that recent rock falls had altered the gully's layout and Calhoun was unable to find the cave paintings a second time. But, even though they didn't find the drawings, the other members of the party also felt Calhoun's sense of dread and felt that a malevolent force was watching them from the shadows.

The unnamed gully of the Porcupine Mountains wasn't the only spot with devilish pictographs found in Michigan. In the 1950s, a group out walking in the woods stumbled across another interesting find at the aptly named Corpse Pond. In a little clearing they found a conspicuous stone standing in the center of the clearing. Getting closer to inspect the strange stone, the hikers discovered macabre depictions of little men in the process of devouring a larger one. On the same stone were also crude depictions of the constellations as well. Like Calhoun fifty years earlier, they too felt like they were being watched and decided to leave in a hurry. Also, like Calhoun, they later returned to the sight to study the drawings again. Though they knew they were near Corpse Pond, strangely enough, they could find neither the rock nor the clearing it had stood in. They had disappeared, almost as if by magic.

Sources:

Curran, Dr. Bob and Ian Daniels. *American Vampires: Their True Bloody History From New York to California.* Weiser, 2012.

STILL FROM NOSFERATU (1922).

CHAPTER 21
NOSFERATU OF NEW YORK

On November 2, 1870, the *Indianapolis Journal* published what is certainly one of the most lurid—and also totally forgotten—real vampire tales of our time. It took place in New York City and centered on a vampiric man only identified as Long:

A HUMAN VAMPIRE.
The Latest New York Sensation.

The New York Star has found a human vampyre at the boarding house of a Mrs. Hunter on East Fourteenth street. From a three-column account we extract:

THE BOOKSELLER's CLERK, LONG

This Long was a singular looking creature. Of moderate height, he was thin and angular everywhere save in his abdomen. This protruded like a round, bloated bag, in a dropsical manner. His hands were long and ivory white. The nails were bitten, and a ragged growth of reddish hair, something like rusty moss, grew on his fingers. His face was perpetually livid, while his eyes were dull and corpse-like. His hair was a dingy brick-red, his eye-brows almost colorless, and his eye lashes totally absent. He stooped and never looked boldly into anyone's face. His lips, of a dull purple tint and ragged-edged, protruded considerably. His voice was hoarse and husky. He seldom spoke. He never sat out of his own room except at meal times. He never smoked. He never took part in the amusements, such as they were, of the parlor. He kept coldly to himself, and his appearance was so repulsive that no one ever attempted to establish an intimacy with him. He was almost singular enough in his behavior to be deemed mad.

He was full of strange tricks. One day Mrs. Hunter, in carving, cut her finger. At once he sprang from his seat, savagely seized the bleeding member and thrust it into his mouth, slobbering his face over with blood. Then suddenly leaping to the door he made his escape. Mrs. Hunter took it as a tribute of uncouth affection, and smiled, afterwards, as she told the story. He loved raw meat. He would stop in front of butchers' shops and watch with watering mouth the dismemberment of cattle and sheep, buying now and then a bleeding handful of fibre, which he used to chew with avidity. He was always catting his fingers, and it was noticed that whenever he did so, he would lap up the blood that flowed from his wound, with ravenous delight. These and a dozen such instances of depravity made those who knew him loathe and detest him.

The young Doctor, full of hygienic theories, tried hard, but tried vainly, to connect the sickness so prevalent in the house with imperfect drainage or some other *reison d'etre* of half the maladies in the world. All attempts of the kind failed. He could not reconcile the symptoms with miasmatic influences, and he gave up in despair the solution of the problem with any theory of this sort for a primary assumption.

But he was destined to penetrate the mystery. One fine evening there had been an interesting autopsy on a case of complicated disease. The Doctor had been present and had taken an active share in the post mortem researches incidental to such an event. A young surgeon from Blackwell's Island had also "assisted" at the dissection. The hour at which the medical conclave adjourned was so late that the Blackwell's Island Doctor was compelled to accept an offer on the part of our friend of Twenty-fourth street & share his room for the rest of the night. The visitor gladly complied

COWBOYS & VAMPIRES

with his friends invitation, and at about midnight the two physicians retired, carefully bolting their door. Exhausted by their scientific labors, they soon fell asleep. The young police doctor woke at about 2 o'clock in the morning, and feeling the heat very keenly, opened his door and went in search of some ice water. He fancied he heard footsteps noiselessly straying about the house, but doubting the possibility of any felonious intrusion on the premises, he resolutely determined that the sound was purely imaginary. He was gone some time. When he entered his apartment he confronted

A SPECTACLE OF GHASTLY HORROR.

His friend was lying fast asleep, with the moonlight steeping his pale face in its silver flood of radiance. The slumberer's eyes were closed. His chest heaved with the flow of life. His lips were parted in an unconscious smile, and the lines of care and work were smoothed, as if by magic, out of his wan young face. Crouched on the man's body, his eyes bright with an un natural brilliancy, was the live corpse, Long. His white hands were buried up to their wrists in the pillows. He had nothing but his shirt to cover his nakedness, and his long attenuated legs made him fearfully like a hogs white spider. His throat swelled and collapsed, as he steadily sucked at a spot under the sleeper's ear. A low purring sound mingled with the lapping of his victim's blood. His fiendish eyes glared into the other's white face. His baggy stomach wagged from side to side in ecstasy. His sleek white back and breast shone in the moonlight, and his red hair bristled up with angry erectness. As he sucked the other grew whiter and weaker. Lovely visions seemed to take the place of his life's blood. As the monster drank in the precious fluid, the smile that hovered about his lips grew softer and sweeter. It was just the opposite with the murderer. The draught of blood seemed to intoxicate him. He swelled with it. It flashed red and fiery out of his eyes. It crimsoned his ghastly face. It thickens his thin fingers and made his arms round and easy. The monster grew less hideous and more devilish with every drop.

Our friend could stand the awful scene no longer. With a yell of rage and with a conviction that the evil genius of the house stood at last revealed, he sprang upon the Vampire. The demon, yelling like a hyena and mad with the frenzy of blood seized him with his teeth. The fight was desperate. The Vampire tore his adversary's arm and growled like a savage beast as he drank from fresh veins. The surgeon felt in his coat pocket for some instrument. He found a small lancet and with it stabbed the monster in the shoulder. The blood spurted out and splashed over the third participant in this awful tragedy, who still slept the sleep of exhaustion. With a ghoulish yell the Vampire tried to fasten his hot pouting lips on the wound from which his own life-blood was flowing. The combat was desperately brief. One last hopeless effort of the doctor drove the Vampire's head against the door post, and he fell stunned. Sinking on the bed the doctor called for aid. Two gentlemen, sinking home from a night's dissipation heard the cry and came to his assistance.

A terribly

TRAGIC SPECTACLE

greeted their eyes. The young surgeon from Blackwell Island was lying white and corpse-like on the bed. Huge gouts and blotches of blood fouled the linen and discolored his bleached face. The police doctor, in a dead faint, lay half on and half off the bed, with abundant hemorrhage from his wounds. On the floor, breathing stertorously, and quite insensible, was the Vampire, Long. The Vampire was immediately secured, and the two doctors were attended by members of their own profession. They soon recovered.

The incident of this night proved conclusively enough the connection between the mysterious ailment of Mrs. Hunter's boarders and the hideous creature Long. This fearful being was removed to the City Lunatic Asylum, but killed himself soon after his reception by rolling his tongue backward down his throat, thus excluding air from the larynx. This he did on being refused a diet of blood.

DOCTORED STILL OF NOSFERATU (1922).

This creature sounds a bit like the Max Schreck Nosferatu, only with red hair. Did I mistake a penny dreadful for an actual article? I'm not sure if Penny Dreadfuls were ever reprinted in papers as news items, but I would like to note that not only did this story appear on page two of the paper, but it was flanked mostly by advertisements and other very serious, and dare I say very boring, stories. In other words, this story wasn't in the back pages with other strange stories.

I would also like to point out that this story predates *Dracula*. The bit where Long suckled the blood from a cut finger is very much like the scene where Stoker has Dracula lap the blood from Jonathon Harker when he cuts his finger. Did Stoker somehow find this article years later, or is it pure coincidence?

That Long was susceptible to injury and that he committed suicide by choking on his own tongue points more towards demon possession than an immortal vampire, though. (If the story has any truth to it at all, that is.)

CHAPTER 19
THE VAMPIRE QUILT

You've heard of the vampire chair of Tennessee, now how about the vampire quilt? Actually, the bewitched object is better known as the Cussing Coverlet and, like the Vampire Chair, is very much attributed to Appalachian witchcraft. It was common in the Pioneer Era to make patchwork quilts, which would often find themselves draped over wood-framed beds. Often these quilts were works of art, and some of the designers made them extra personal by sewing in a lock of hair, baby clothes or other beloved, old garments. However, while those quilts were made with love, a select few were also made with anger and hate. It was thought that some witches could actually weave a curse into the quilt.

After all, what better item to curse than a coverlet with which someone would wrap themselves in on a cold, lonely night. Shivering while wrapped in the blanket, the spell could then take effect. To weave the spell into the coverlet, the witch might use herbs such as snake root, wild parsnip leaves, or pokeweed to name a few. However, the curse would only fully take effect when it was placed on the bed. After that, it would work in one of two ways. Like the South American Anaconda, it would wrap itself around its victim and squeeze them to death. After the victim was dead, the quilt would flatten itself out to avoid suspicion. However, in the second more vampiric method, the quilt would suck the life out of the user—not always to death, though. Sometimes the sleeper would arise, albeit unusually groggy after suffering some kind of terrible nightmare. If not discarded, over time the cursed quilt might eventually kill them. Or, if not that, leave the victim a shell of their former selves.

Only the most wizened and experienced of the old-timers could spot a spell woven into the fabric. Just as Hispanic culture has curanderas, the Appalachians have similar figures that can be good or bad. Tennessee folklorist Dr. Joseph Sobel wrote of one such figure known as Granny Bacon, who operated out of Blount County. People would seek her help in resolving feuds via supernatural means, which sometimes included Cussing Coverlets. Her Cussing Coverlets were said to be the best at draining the life from a person. They were also said to be beautiful.

Then there is the tale of the Cussing Coverlet of Cade's Cove, Tennessee. Some of the first pioneers there consisted of the Estep family. Mavis, the wife, had an unrelenting phobia of being struck by lightning. She had been born during a thunderstorm, and local lore dictated that one day she would be struck. As such, she wouldn't go near metal during a thunderstorm, not even something as tiny as a sewing needle. She also wouldn't sleep in a metal-framed bed.

It may have been Mavis who made the first-ever Cussing Coverlet. It was so named because she took one of her husband's flannel shirts to make a quilt. The shirt was notorious for her because Basil, the husband, had become angry with her and took to using bad language whilst wearing it. In fact, it was their first-ever marital spat. As such, she called it the Cussing Coverlet.

As time passed, Mavis became ill. On her death bed, she told Basil she didn't mind if he remarried, but if he did, she had two stipulations. The first was to never sell or get rid of any of her quilts. The second was to never place any of her quilts on a metal-framed bed. Well, guess what? Though Basil honored the first request, he didn't heed the second. He remarried to a larger woman about a year later. She was so much larger than Mavis that she found the couple's old bed to be too small, and so they bought a bigger one. One with a metal frame...

One night, Trulie, the new wife, became cold and begged Basil to let her get one Mavis's old quilts. Basil relented, and out of all the quilts, Trulie was most enchanted with the Cussing Coverlet. She awoke in the middle of the night to find a ghostly Mavis leering at her from the foot of the bed. Once the two made eye contact, Mavis began to curse at Trulie, who screamed so loudly that it woke Basil. He dismissed it as a nightmare and the couple went back to sleep. Then, despite it being a calm, clear night, a rogue lightning strike somehow entered the room. Trulie was unharmed, but Basil was burnt to a crisp. Neither Trulie nor anything else in the room was harmed or burned, only Basil. Fearfully, Trulie gave the Cussing Coverlet to one of Basil and Mavis's children, who in turn sold it to a collector. Today, the quilt is supposedly still circulating out there somewhere, perhaps in an antique shop draped over the vampire chair?

Sources:

Barnett, Janet and Randy Russell. *The Granny Curse and Other Ghosts and Legends from East Tennessee*. Blair, 1999.

Curran, Dr. Bob and Ian Daniels. *American Vampires: Their True Bloody History From New York to California*. Weiser, 2012.

CHAPTER 20
THE INVISIBLE VAMPIRE

The following tale was published in the *St. Paul Daily Globe* out of Minnesota on March 20, 1893. Whether or not it is true is debatable, but it's certainly elaborate and lengthy:

CAUGHT A WHAT IS IT.
Thrilling Tale of a Dakota Man at the
Merchants' Hotel.
Encounter with a Mysterious Animal
Unknown to Science.
Final Capture and Disposition of the Unseen
What-You-Call-It.
Arrival of Two Officials Sheds Light on the
Strange Story.

COWBOYS & VAMPIRES

"I have a story which may be of interest to the readers of your paper," said Doctor W.W. McIntyre, of New York, Wednesday afternoon to a GLOBE man as he settled himself back on one of the comfortable seats in the lobby of the Merchants.

"I have just returned from a visit to Bismarck S.D., where I have been making an investigation of one of the most interesting affairs it has been my luck to meet with in the history of my professional career. I have in my possession a cast, made in plaster, of an unearthly creature which was found in a house in the vicinity of Bismarck. I was written to in regard to the existence of the strange 'thing,' and it was alive at the time of my arrival in Bismarck. It died a day or two after I got there. If you care to hear the story, I will tell it to you.

"About three weeks ago a man who lives in Bismarck, or, rather, in the immediate vicinity of that city - I will not give his name, by request from him - rented a house located on a farm twelve miles from the city. He was making plans for living on the farm during the coming summer in company with his wife and family. He went to the farm, accompanied by a friend, for the purpose of seeing that everything was in order, and expected to return in the course of a day or two to Bismarck. His friend was employed in one of the banks of Bismarck, and he took the trip with the expectation of enjoying a hunt for a day or two. They arrived at the house all right in the course of the forenoon, and while the banker, whom I will call John Wilkins as that is not his name, went out to kill some partridges, the other man, whom I will call Allen, went through the house. The building had been furnished in an elegant manner by an Englishman, who started a ranch there, but he had moved away after living there for about a year without giving any excuse for so doing. He left orders with his agent to dispose of the property at any price he could get but did not give any reason for doing so. However, some of the servants had told stories of the house being haunted, and they ascribed the precipitate leaving of the Englishman to this cause. All kinds of stories were in circulation about the mysterious sounds about the house, but Wilkins and Allen, the latter being a physician, did not believe in the supernatural. They laughed at the stories, and called the tellers of the yarns old women, after the custom of the Indians.

"Allen made a trip through the house and found in one of the rooms a quantity of bed clothing, carefully packed away in the drawers of a bureau. He proceeded to make up two beds in adjoining rooms, and then waited for the return of his friend. They cooked supper - all Dakota men can keep their own houses properly - and after a good smoke they retired. Allen took one of the rooms and Wilkins slept in an adjoining room. They were tired and went to sleep almost immediately after touching their pillows.

"Allen was awakened during the night by a strange sensation. He could not see anything, as the room was dark, but he felt that there was something in the room. A strange and uncanny feeling took possession of him, and the cold perspiration stood out on his forehead in large drops. It was not a man; he could feel that, but it was some unearthly presence which he could not help but know was there. He sat up in bed, tried to light a candle which he knew must be there, but his hands shook so that he could not find the matches. He was frightened, very much so, although he was known as a brave man, and had been in more than one personal combat during the early days of the settlement of the Dakotas. Suddenly he felt that something was coming near to him. He could feel that something was in his immediate vicinity, when suddenly somebody dropped onto his breast. The feeling of the thing was cold and clammy. It was not very large, but it was possessed of an immense and superhuman strength. The skinny fingers seized his throat with a death grip, and he was at first powerless. The feeling that he was dealing with something of an unnatural form unnerved him, but as he felt his breath being stopped by the pressure of the fingers of the being on his windpipe he was aroused to a sense of his danger, he threw off the lethargy which seized his muscles, and gave a shout for help. He seized the skinny hands which clasped his neck and tried with all his strength to loosen their grip. Finally, after a terrible struggle he gained the mastery of the strange being, and, clasping the wrists of the creature in his hands, he waited for the arrival of his friend, whom he could hear stirring in an adjoining room. Soon the door opened, and Wilkins stepped into the room.

"My God, have you got a fit?" he asked, as he held his candle in the air above his head and peered at Allen. The candle gave a good light in the room, and Allen looked at the creature which had tried to choke him. Horrors! There was nothing there. Nothing which he could see, although he could feel the struggles of the thing and hear its breath. His fingers clasped something and the forms of the wrists which he held could be seen in the air, but, to his eyes, nothing was there.

"'Get something so that I can tie it,' he gasped, as he was almost out of breath from struggling.

"'Tie what?' asked Wilkins with a laugh. 'You had better go back to bed as you are dreaming.'

"'But I am not. Can't you see where my fingers were clasping something. It can't be seen, but there is something there. My God, man, I am not crazy. Look at the bites on my arms and wrists where this creature has bitten me. Feel of it yourself.'

"Wilkins stepped up to his friend for a moment and put his hand out towards where the creature was. He suddenly withdrew his hand with a cry of pain, and the red blood spurted out of his hand. He had been bitten.

"They took one of the sheets from the bed and tied it around the arms and legs of the creature. Then the body was laid on the bed. It was a strange sight. There could be seen the folds of the sheet as they were wound around the body. The twists and turns which had been given were all there, but they seemed to surround nothing but air. On the pillow and bed clothing could be seen the outlines of something which pressed into them in the form of a child, but no body could be seen. The panting of the captured thing could be heard, exhausted with its struggle, and if the hand was placed in the vicinity of its mouth the snap of teeth could be heard. It had lungs, the form of a human being, and on touching it the same sensation as of contact with a dead person could be felt. It made no sound and did not utter a cry during the entire struggle.

"The remainder of the night was spent in sitting by the side of the bed and watching the movements of the wrappings. They could not imagine what it was or what it could be, as Allen, the doctor, had never heard of anything of the kind. When morning came, they wrapped it up in several blankets and took it to the office of the doctor. They wondered if it could eat, or if it desired to eat anything. Food was offered, but it would not partake of it. Allen then wired for me, as he knew I was interested in freaks of nature and all kinds of queer things. I started at once for Bismarck and arrived as soon as the train could take me there.

"I found everything as had been represented in the short dispatch which I had received. We examined it from every standpoint, but I could make nothing out of it. It was decided that it would be proper for us to preserve it in the interests of science, but the question was how could we do it? Finally, a happy idea was hit upon. It had a form which, although it could not be seen, could be felt. Why not make a plaster cast of it. We decided to do this, but as we were afraid of killing the creature by taking a cast while it was alive, we decided to try the effects of chloroform on it.

"We succeeded. The chloroform which we administered put it into a deep sleep, and we took the cast. But on removing the plaster we found that it had stopped breathing. We were unable to resuscitate it in anyway, and after keeping the body for some time it was buried in the woods in a carefully marked spot.

"I shall present the cast to the Smithsonian institute after it has been examined by my friends in New York. Quite a yarn, isn't it? I supposed people will think I have been drinking some of the North Dakota whisky, but it is true, every word of it.

"The cast? That has been shipped by express to New York."

As the doctor concluded his narration two muscular men, with the air of officers stepped up to the doctor, and one of them tapped him on the shoulder.

"Better go to bed and get some rest," he said, and the doctor quietly went up the stairs accompanied by one of them.

"A good fellow, but...

He tapped his forehead in a significant manner and then followed the doctor and his companion. They left on the evening train for New York. The doctor had escaped three weeks before and was found in Fargo.

There are two ways to view this story. One, every bit of it was made up. But, on that note, everyone hates stories that turn out to be dreams or delusions, so if that was the case, why bother? Option Two, the story was true and an escaped mental patient who thinks himself a doctor told a wild story to a reporter. In that case, there's a hole in the story in the sense that this escaped mental patient was left alone in a room with another man. If he was an escapee, I highly doubt he would be left alone. Option Three, the story is true, but... what if the doctor wasn't an escaped inmate? What if he really was a doctor who told of his discovery to the press? What if the two men with him were something akin to the Men in Black and this was their simple, easy solution to the problem of the chatty doctor?

Also odd is the time and place of this story, as it predated the South Dakota/Nebraska vampire tale by three years. And, after all, in some folklore, vampires can turn invisible just like ghosts...

CHAPTER 22
VANISHING VIRGINIA VAMPIRE

Long before the better-known and probably entirely folkloric Richmond Vampire, Virginia played host to yet another vampire. Predating the Church Hill Tunnel incident, this vampiric encounter occurred back in the late 1800s in Big Stone Gap in Wise County along the Tennessee and Kentucky border. (Sources won't list an exact date other than that it pre-dated the 1897 publication of *Dracula*.)

The case began with a rash of mysterious cattle mutilations. Had these same mutilations occurred one hundred years later, aliens would have been blamed. The cattle, or what was left of them, were completely drained of blood. Parts of them had been drug away, leaving only the head and hind quarters behind. At first, only two cows were found by a local farmer. This was soon followed by three other farms losing their cattle to similar conditions.

Since this was the Victorian Era, bloodsuckers were blamed as opposed to aliens, and a meeting of the area patriarchs at a local tavern determined that a vampire was to blame. When it came down to singling out culprits, the prime suspect was a reclusive man who lived in a remote cabin known only as Mr. Rupp. The timing couldn't have been more perfect in their minds since the strange mutilations began right around the time that Rupp moved to the area.

And, if two peeping toms are to be believed, Rupp really was an eater of raw meat even if he wasn't a vampire. Two local boys peered through his cabin window one day and saw him gnawing on a large chunk of raw meat in front of his fireplace. Were the boys just making things up to add fuel to the fire of the rumors they'd no doubt heard? A local sheriff considered that as a possibility considering that he refused to arrest Mr. Rupp without conclusive evidence. Not to mention, there was no crime against eating raw meat, even if it was unusual, nor could it be proven that the raw meat came from one of the dead cattle.

Things became more ominous when the town drunk went missing and was later found only a quarter-mile away from Rupp's cabin. He was missing an arm and a leg and had also been drained of blood just like the cattle! Following the town drunk was a traveling salesman found the exact same way.

Just like in the old Universal horror movies, the locals formed an angry mob and marched to Rupp's cabin. Rupp wasn't there, and when they barged in, they found a grizzly abode of severed limbs and body parts from humans and animals alike. Even the tabletops were drenched in blood. The smell from the interior was so bad that several ran outside and vomited. The townsfolk set fire to the abominable cabin, and the memory of it was said to haunt those that saw it for the rest of their lives.

Though a search party looked diligently for the vampire, Mr. Rupp was never found. Some speculated that he died alone in the woods, but if that were so, his body was never found. That said, Rupp's ghost is said to haunt the woods to this day, and mysterious deaths and disappearances are blamed on the vampire. Some who have tried to determine the veracity of this folktale state that it didn't make any newspapers that can be found, but that doesn't mean that it didn't happen.

Some also argue that Rupp was merely a cannibal. If that was so, how did he drain the animals' blood? If he didn't drink it, then blood should have littered the ground where the animals were killed. True vampire or not, it appears that Rupp was indeed a bonafide bloodsucker.

Sources:

Schlosser, S.E. *Spooky Virginia: Tales of Hauntings, Strange Happenings and Other Local Lore.* Globe Pequot, 2010.

Thompson, Hope. "Appalachian Folklife: The Mysterious Vampire of Big Stone Gap." Unmasked History Magazine (September 25, 2019) https://unmaskedhistory.com/2019/09/25/appalachian-folklife-the-mysterious-vampire-of-big-stone-gap/

CHAPTER 23
BUCKETS OF BLOOD

Our next vampire tale took place in California but was printed in the *Fort Worth Gazette* on August 13, 1891:

A HUMAN VAMPIRE. A MAN WHO HAS DRANK A BUCKET OF HUMAN
BLOOD, Several Victims Have Disappeared and Never Been Accounted for
Drinks Dog's Blood When he Can't Get Man's

Special to the Gazette.
MOUNTAIN VIEW. Cal., Aug. 5.—There is lying in jail here a man who, if his own statement deserves credence, has drunk a bucket of human blood. It is believed that not less than

A HUMAN VAMPIRE.

A MAN WHO HAS DRANK A BUCKET OF HUMRN BLOOD.

Several Victims Have Disappeared and Never Been Accounted for—Drinks Dog's Blood When he Can't Get Man's.

Special to the Gazette.

MOUNTAIN VIEW, CAL., Aug. 5.—There is lying in jail here a man who, if his own statement deserves credence, has drunk a bucket of human blood. It is believed that not less than twenty men have met death at his hands in order to satisfy his desire to drink the life-giving fluid fresh from their veins. This man, Illario Ortego, a Malay, is now serving a six month's sentence in the county jail for threatening the life of Alexander Morphy, a ranchman on Steven's creek. This human vampire is a Manilla Malay, and his whole appearance is most revolting. The fierce brute passion shines from his eyes, which flash and sparkle under deep, overhanging brows, the hair of which grows together in the center and hangs in a tuft down over the bridge of his nose. His flat nostrils are expanded and quiver convulsively as he talks of the past. His thin lips are drawn tight and partly disclose a set of wolfish teeth. His hair stands erect

twenty men have met death at his hands in order to satisfy his desire to drink the life-giving fluid fresh from their veins. This man, Illario Ortego, a Malay, is now serving a six month sentence in the county jail for threatening the life of Alexander Morphy, a ranchman on Steven's creek. This human vampire is a Manilla Malay, and his whole appearance is most revolting. The fierce brute passion shines from his eyes, which flash and sparkle under deep, overhanging brows, the hair of which grows together in the center and hangs in a tuft down over the bridge of his nose. His flat nostrils are expanded and quiver convulsively as he talks of his frightful acts of the past. His thin lips are drawn tight and partly disclose a set of wolfish teeth. His hair stands erect and his small, pointed ears lie flat and close to his skull. His body is misshapen, supported by distorted legs, while his long, slender hands clutch convulsively at the ends of knotted and gnarled arms. A more repulsive appearing human being could scarcely be conceived.

He first appeared in this country in 1860. Whenever he formed an enmity towards a man he would follow him until his vengeance was satisfied, but if this was long delayed he would kill a dog and drink its blood while it flowed, yet warm from the veins. Soon after his arrival he killed a bed-mate, named Manilla Juan, and for this he was convicted and sent to the penitentiary for fifteen years. He was released in 1875 and celebrated his release by trying to murder an old companion named Clementi, who had assisted him in burying Juan. He failed in the attempt, but a few days later Clementi disappeared, but he was of such a character that no one took the trouble to investigate his taking off. Illario's next escapade was chasing Thomas Besanti over the country and shooting at him with a rifle. He was tried for attempted murder and was acquitted. He then cursed the judge from the dock for not sending him to San Quentin prison, as he said it was much easier living there than on Steven's creek. Shortly after this, Illario said that he was getting old and needed a drink of blood to make him young again. He was prevented from killing a man known as French Ben, but Ben soon after disappeared and no trace of him was found.

Last March two young men named Morphy moved into the neighborhood. The younger of the boys looked to the Malay like a fit victim, and on meeting him on the road he began telling the boy how easy it would be to put a knife into him and how good his blood would taste. He danced around the boy, swinging his hat in his face and saying that that was the way he stabbed people. The boy told him to put on his hat and he would show him how a white man did it. The Malay put his hat on and the boy drew his revolver and fired all his shots through it except one. He then told Illario to go home, which he did, cursing the boy. To make his vow of vengeance more binding, he killed a dog and drank its blood. Before an opportunity arose to kill Morphy, the boy left the country, and the Malay determined to kill his brother. He openly said he would kill him and drink his blood. He took a wooden bucket, and said that he had already drank enough to fill it and wanted more. It was while lying in wait for Morphy that he was arrested. The keepers at the jail say that he delights in catching rats, and will bite their heads off while they are yet alive and suck their blood.

The last bit of the story intrigues me because it sounds very much like Renfield, the fly-eating madman from Bram Stoker's *Dracula*. Was this yet another article that Stoker collected, or is it simply another instance of art imitating life? That's difficult to say, but this individual certainly sounds more like a madman who thinks himself a vampire as opposed to an immortal murderer. It was intriguing, though, that this man knew of the belief that ingesting blood could rejuvenate him.

POSTSCRIPT
THE
VAMPIRE'S
GRAVE

Much like the Lafayette "vampire" of Colorado is the "vampire" of a small graveyard in Dalby Springs, Bowie County, Texas. Cedar Grove Cemetery, aptly named, is tucked away in a tree grove and is well hidden.[38] It's far off the beaten path and can only be reached via a bumpy old wagon trail. The small cemetery boasts only about 20 graves and was first used in the mid-1800s, and the last burial took place in 1903.

---

[38] The first church there was built in 1839, so presumably that's when the graveyard sprouted as well. Also, the cemetery was originally known as Pleasant Grove Cemetery.

At the back of the cemetery is the "Vampire's Grave," so-called because it lacks a name and is very, very spooky. The plot is six by eight feet in dimensions, and the gate is six feet high. The grave is fenced in and has an iron stake driven right in the middle of it. Or at least it used to. The iron gate has been removed due to adventurous teenagers entering the cage—presumably due to the vampire legend—and getting trapped within it. The stake, too, has since been taken away, possibly out of fear of someone injuring themselves on it.[39] Or maybe a souvenir hunter dislodged it in hopes of resurrecting the alleged vampire. In any case, local lore held that the stake was a bit like Excalibur, as all teens who did their best to remove it failed.

There's another strange detail about the burial plot. Allegedly, for a time, there were two torches located at the grave. In her article on the Dalby Vampire for *The East Texas Journal*, Greta Reeves quoted a source who claimed that "there were two flame holders atop two poles of the fence, at the back of the 'cage.'" And that "the flames burned throughout several nights of the year until they were stolen, taken away."[40] Who lit these flames and kept them going all night is still a mystery.

Another strange detail was dropped by the same source, stating that the grave ran on a north to south line, the opposite of a traditional Christian burial. This was done, she said, so that the vampire

---

[39] It was last seen sometime around the year 2000.
[40] Reeves, "Vampire Legend Haunts Dalby Springs Back Road," *East Texas Journal*.

wouldn't see the Lord approaching on Judgement Day per traditions of the era.

CEDAR GROVE CEMETERY, WITH VAMPIRE'S GRAVE IN BACKGROUND.

To better understand the vampire, we should first delve into the history of the area where it is buried. Dalby Springs began in the 1830s upon the arrival of the Warren Dalby family, who discovered springs on their property known for their mineral content. The mineral-rich water quickly became known for its medicinal properties, thus leading to the construction of housing for those seeking its health benefits in the 1850s. By 1860, a post office followed, and in the mid-1880s, the population reached its peak with 250 people. By the early

1900s, people began to learn of better cures for their ailments and quit coming to the area. At some point, the original church burnt down in the early 1900s and was later rebuilt. Today, the church still stands and about 100 residents or so remain in the area.

DALBY SPRINGS METHODIST CHURCH. BUILT OF KNOTLESS PINE LUMBER IN 1888. FIRST HOUSE OF WORSHIP BUILT BY CONGREGATION WHO HAD BEEN WORSHIPPING SINCE 1839 IN HOMES, GROVES AND SCHOOL. DURING THIS TIME THE TOWN OF DALBY SPRINGS EMERGED FROM FARMLAND AND GREW INTO A SUMMER HEALTH SPA. RECORDED TEXAS HISTORIC LANDMARK — 1966

DALBY SPRINGS HISTORICAL MARKER.

But why the legend of the vampire? Did the unmarked grave perhaps belong to someone suffering from tuberculosis à la Mercy Brown? Or could the vampire legend stem from the waters themselves? A quote from a Jesse Suttles on TexasLegends.com mentions that at one point the waters of Dalby Springs were actually red! This was in the 1950s and Suttles said, "The water from the well was dark red. It didn't smell very good. If you put the water in a glass jug, over time the inside of the jug would turn a dark rusty color. I guess it was from sulfur in the water or another mineral."[41]

---

41 http://www.texasescapes.com/EastTexasTowns/Dalby-Springs-Texas.htm

Greta Reeves may have found a more logical explanation in her research. Though she can't be certain that this was the name on the unmarked vampire's grave, she did find an entry of an Eliziz Williams born in 1797 and buried at Cedar Grove on October 31, 1879. Perhaps children simply saw the death date and decided the woman must have been a vampire? (Conversely, Texas Gravestone.org identifies the birthdate for Eliziz Williams as October 31, 1797, and she died on March 10, 1879.) And, Reeves did manage to find a grave for a Mrs. Williams (first name illegible) right next to the spot where the iron fence used to be. Another source told Reeves that all the burial records burned with the first church and that she believed the vampire legend was created by a caretaker to scare away possible vandals. (The logic in this is somewhat flawed, as stories of a vampire are instead what would likely draw vandals and thrill-seekers!) [42]

Just as I was about to label the case of the Texas Vampire a tall tale with no real supernatural activity to back it up, I came across the work of paranormal researcher Melba Goodwyn, who visited the cemetery on several occasions, and on two of them, very strange things happened. In her book, *Ghost*

---

[42] The cemetery is quite hard to find and is apparently mistaken for the Red Hill Cemetery south of the town of New Boston, twelve miles away from Cedar Grove Cemetery. Ironically, Red Hill Cemetery has its own "vampire" or ghost that is said to repose in a mausoleum. But it's thought this tale was inspired by Cedar Grove's vampire.

Worlds, Goodwyn recounted seeing a white fog enshroud the grave and experiencing paralyses at the grave before she snapped out of it and fled the cemetery. She was with her daughter, who claimed she could hear beautiful harp music coming from near the grave. She grabbed her mother's hand in a strong, steely grasp and tried to drag her into the white fog. Goodwyn managed to snap her daughter out of it and take her back to the car so they could leave. Later in the car, her daughter had the "missing time" experience common to alien abductions and fairy encounters in that she could not remember the incident at all.

Sometime later, Goodwyn brought a whole team of fellow paranormal investigators with her to study the grave. Her book *Chasing Graveyard Ghosts* provides one of the best write-ups on the vampire ever. According to Goodwyn, one will feel an unsettling chill the moment they walk into the cemetery, which she notes is on the 33rd parallel. Just as aliens and ghosts have a penchant for showing up at 3:30 A.M., strange things tend to occur on the 33rd parallel more so than others. Roswell, New Mexico, is located along this line as is Mt. Hermon in the Holy Land, where angels descended from the skies during the days of Enoch. Due to being situated on the 33rd parallel, it is even rumored that the upper-echelon, more occult driven Masons use the vampire's grave for arcane rituals.

Contrary to theories that the vampire story was made up by local teenagers—or elderly caretakers hoping to scare teenagers away—Goodwyn stated that she found quite a few elderly residents who do indeed believe the vampire story and are reluctant to talk about it, as if it's taboo. It was Goodwyn who brought the EVP and recorded the startling voice mentioned earlier. She also reported that a glowing red orb with menacing "eyes" was sighted. They could also hear the flapping of unseen wings somewhere as well. Eventually the terror mounted until Goodwyn and her team literally ran from the cemetery.

Goodwyn also claimed that the grave isn't the burial site of one vampire, but a whole family. Goodwyn postulated an imaginative theory as to what would bring the vampires to the area. While I had earlier mused that perhaps someone with a blood disease had begotten the vampire rumors, Goodwyn wondered if vampires moved to the health resort to take advantage of all the ill people there. After all, they would be too weak to ward them off, and when they died, it wouldn't be unexpected since they were ill. Goodwyn further went on to wonder if the removal of the stake removed the vampire or vampires plural? She wondered if the removal of the stake was why the place felt so haunted when she and her team investigated the area.

Though she doesn't give an exact source (presumably a local told her), she says that in the late 1800s a family of foreigners moved into the area. None of them, except for the father, could speak English, and his was very limited. For whatever reason, the family was suspected of being vampires and they were murdered and then buried in the cemetery, or so the story goes.

In recent years, a YouTube user, SafariClubUSA, uploaded a video of the cemetery. In the comments below, one user, Teresa Lynn, mentioned how the corners of the grave had upside-down crosses on them![43] The cage as it appears in the video is definitely creepy too. In 2010, SafariClubUSA made a nighttime visit to Cedar Grove Cemetery and filmed some mysterious bones near the grave. When they returned in the daylight to get a better idea of what the bones were, they were gone. Like the Lafayette Vampire, a recording was taken one night by a paranormal investigator, and the voice allegedly could be heard saying, "Come to the end of the row where the dead plague the living."

Though the simplest explanation is that people simply made up the vampire tale, you also have to ask yourself, why in the world would someone drive a metal stake right in the middle of an unmarked grave? You have to admit, it does make you wonder...

[43] SafariClubUSA, Vampire in Texas?, August 23, 2009.
https://www.youtube.com/watch?v=rk1zvBmdh1Y

THE UNDEAD IN NORTH AMERICA

Sources:

Goodwyn, Melba. *Chasing Graveyard Ghosts: Investigations of Haunted & Hallowed Ground.* Llewellyn Publications, 2011

------------------------------ *Ghost Worlds: A Guide to Poltergeists, Portals, Ecto-Mist, & Spirit Behavior.* Llewellyn Publications, 2007.

Reeves, Greta. "Vampire Legend Haunts Dalby Springs Back Road." *East Texas Journal* (July 12, 2018)

SafariClubUSA. "Vampire in Texas?" August 23, 2009. https://www.youtube.com/watch?v=rkIzvBmdh1Y

INDEX

Anam Paranormal, 78-79

Battle of Chickamauga, 93, 107-110

Bigfoot, 108

Brown, George, 21-30

Brown, James, 135-142

Brown, Mercy, 21-30, 137, 184

Cade's Cove, Tennessee, 163

Cagliostro, 64

Carmilla, 13

Casket Girls, 57-58

Čečar, Milo, 12

Chonchon, 101

Chupacabra, 14, 104

Church Hill, Virginia, 127-131

Crow Nation, 111-115

Curse of the Undead, 31

Cussing Coverlet, 161-164

Dalby Springs, Texas, 181-189

de Soto, Hernando, 111

Dracula, 12, 14, 16, 18, 20-21, 30-32, 77, 135, 137, 159, 173, 180

Exeter, Rhode Island, 14, 21-30, 135

Germain, Jacques/Comte, 57-66

Glava, Todor, 76-77

Great Lakes, 149-151

Green Eyes, 107-110

Guadalajara, Mexico, 103

Horror of Dracula, 14

Jewett vampires, 22

Johnson, Andrew, 138-139

Keel, John, 84, 87

Lafayette, Colorado, 75-79, 181, 188

Le Fanu, Sheridan, 13

Lillith, 11, 55

Livingston County, Missouri, 67

Mapuche sorcerers, 101

Mineral Point Vampire, 81-87

Moon Eyed People, 88-94, 112

Mothman, 84, 87

Mount Shasta, 66

Nebraska Vampire, 31-43

New Orleans, Louisiana, 57-60 64, 66

Nimerigar, 116

Nirumbee, 112, 116

Nosferatu, 130-131, 141-142, 159

Nukekubi, 100

Nunez, Alvaro, 91

Nutini, Hugo, 55-56

Odom, Eli and Jacob, 120, 124

Pine Ridge territory, 31-43

Plenty Coups, 113-115

Point Pleasant, West Virginia, 84

Polidori, John, 13

Pool, W.W., 128-131

Pryor Mountains, 114

Richmond Vampire, 127-
132, 173
Ridgeway Phantom, 81-
87
Romania, 21
Roswell, New Mexico,
186
Savanović, Sava, 12
Sioux City, Iowa, 40-42
skinwalkers, 120
Slagle, Joseph, 67-74
Sobel, Dr. Joseph, 162

Stoker, Bram, 12-13, 15,
21, 30, 32-33, 137, 160,
180
tlahuelpuchi, 47, 48, 50,
51, 52, 53, 54, 55, 56
Tlahuelpuchi, 45-56, 104
Tlaxcala, Mexico, 45-56
Trandafir, John, 76-78
Transylvania, 21, 64, 76-
77
Vampyre, The, 13
Vlad the Impaler, 21
werewolf, 15, 47

ABOUT THE AUTHOR

John LeMay was born and raised in Roswell, NM, the "UFO Capital of the World." He is the author of over 35 books on film and western history such as *Kong Unmade: The Lost Films of Skull Island*, *Tall Tales and Half Truths of Billy the Kid*, and *Roswell USA: Towns That Celebrate UFOs, Lake Monsters, Bigfoot and Other Weirdness*. In addition to non-fiction, he is also the author of the novel *The Noted Desperado Pancho Dumez*. He is also the editor/publisher of *The Lost Films Fanzine* and has written for magazines such as *True West, Cinema Retro,* and *Mad Scientist* to name only a few. He is a Past President of the Board of Directors for the Historical Society for Southeast New Mexico and the host of the web series *Roswell's Hidden History*.

THE BICEP BOOKS CATALOGUE

The following titles are available for purchase on Amazon.com, and are available to bookstores at a wholesale discount via Ingram Content Group (ISBNs of available editions listed for this purpose)

THE BIG BOOK OF JAPANESE GIANT MONSTER MOVIES SERIES

The third edition of the book that started it all! Reviews over 100 tokusatsu films between 1954 and 1988. All the Godzilla, Gamera, and Daimajin movies made during the Showa era are covered plus lesser known fare like *Invisible Man vs. The Human Fly* (1957) and *Conflagration* (1975). Softcover (380 pp/5.83" X 8.27") Suggested Retail: $19.99 SBN:978-1-7341546-4-1

This third edition reviews over 75 tokusatsu films between 1989 and 2019. All the Godzilla, Gamera, and Ultraman movies made during the Heisei era are covered plus independent films like *Reigo, King of the Sea Monsters* (2005), *Demeking, the Sea Monster* (2009) and *Attack of the Giant Teacher* (2019)! Softcover (260 pp/5.83" X 8.27") Suggested Retail: $19.99 ISBN: 978-1- 7347816-4-9

This second edition of the Rondo Award nominated book covers un-produced scripts like *Bride of Godzilla* (1955), partially shot movies like *Giant Horde Beast Nezura* (1963), and banned films like *Proph-ecies of Nostradamus* (1974), plus hundreds of other lost productions. Soft-cover/Hard-cover (470pp. /7" X 10") Suggested Retail: $24.99 (sc)/$39.95(hc)ISBN: 978-1-73 41546-0-3 (hc)

This sequel to *The Lost Films* covers the non-giant monster unmade movie scripts from Japan such as *Frankenstein vs. the Human Vapor* (1963), *After Japan Sinks* (1974-76), plus lost movies like *Fearful Attack of the Flying Saucers* (1956) and *Venus Flytrap* (1968). Hardcover (200 pp/5.83" X 8.27")/Softcover (216 pp/ 5.5" X 8.5") Suggested Retail: $9.99 (sc)/$24.99(hc) ISBN:978-1-7341546 -3-4 (hc)

This companion book to *The Lost Films* charts the development of all the prominent Japanese monster movies including discarded screenplays, story ideas, and deleted scenes. Also includes bios for writers like Shinichi Sekizawa, Niisan Takahashi and many others. Comprehensive script listing and appendices as well. Hard-cover/Softcover (370 pp./ 6"X9") Suggested Retail: $16.95(sc)/$34.99(hc)ISBN: 978-1-7341546-5-8 (hc)

Examines the differences between the U.S. and Japanese versions of over 50 different tokusatsu films like *Gojira* (1954)/*Godzilla, King of the Monsters!* (1956), *Gamera* (1965)/ *Gammera, the Invincible* (1966), *Submersion of Japan* (1973)/*Tidal Wave* (1975), and many, many more! Softcover (540 pp./ 6"X9") Suggested Retail: $22.99 ISBN: 978-1-953221-77 -3

Examines the differences between the European and Japanese versions of tokusatsu films including the infamous "Cozzilla" col-orized version of *Godzilla*, from 1977, plus rarities like *Terremoto 10 Grado*, the Italian cut of *Legend of Dinosaurs*. The book also examines the condensed Champion Matsuri edits of Toho's effects films. Softcover (372 pp./ 6"X9") Suggested Retail: $19.99 ISBN: 978-1- 953221-77-3

Throughout the 1960s and 1970s the Italian film industry cranked out over 600 "Spaghetti Westerns" and for every *Fistful of Dollars* were a dozen pale imitations, some of them hilarious. Many of these lesser known Spaghettis are available in bargain bin DVD packs and stream for free online. If ever you've wondered which are worth your time and which aren't, this is the book for you. Softcover (160pp./5.06" X 7.8") Suggested Retail: $9.99

THE BICEP BOOKS CATALOGUE

Kong Unmade explores unproduced scripts like *King Kong vs. Frankenstein* (1958), unfinished films like *The Lost Island* (1934), and lost movies like *King Kong Appears in Edo* (1938). As a bonus, all the Kong rip-offs like *Konga* (1961) and *Queen Kong* (1976) are reviewed. Hardcover (350 pp/5.83" X 8.27")/Softcover (376 pp/ 5.5" X 8.5") Suggested Retail: $24.99 (hc)/$19.99(sc) ISBN: 978-1-7341546-2-7(hc)

Jaws Unmade explores unproduced scripts like *Jaws 3, People 0* (1979), abandoned ideas like a Quint prequel, and even aborted sequels to Jaws inspired movies like *Orca Part II*. As a bonus, all the Jaws rip-offs like *Grizzly* (1976) and *Tentacles* (1977) are reviewed. Hardcover (316 pp/5.83" X 8.27")/Softcover (340 pp/5.5" X 8.5") Suggested Retail: $29.99 (hc)/$17.95(sc) ISBN: 978-1-7344730-1-8

Classic Monsters Unmade covers lost and unmade films starring Dracula, Frankenstein, the Mummy and more monsters. Reviews unmade scripts like *The Return of Frankenstein* (1934) and *Wolf Man vs. Dracula* (1944). It also examines lost films of the silent era such as *The Werewolf* (1913) and *Drakula's Death* (1923). Softcover/ Hardcover(428pp/5.83"X8.27") Suggested Retail: $22.99(sc)/ $27.99(hc)ISBN:978-1-953221-85-8(hc)

Volume 2 explores the Hammer era and beyond, from unmade versions of *Brides of Dracula* (called *Disciple of Dracula*) to remakes of *Creature from the Black Lagoon*. Completely unmade films like *Kali: Devil Bride of Dracula* (1975) and *Godzilla vs. Frankenstein* (1964) are covered along with lost completed films like *Batman Fights Dracula* (1967) and *Black the Ripper* (1974). Coming Fall 2021.

Written in the same spirit as *The Big Book of Japanese Giant Monster Movies*, this tome reviews all the classic Universal and Hammer horrors to star Dracula, Frankenstein, the Gillman and the rest along with obscure flicks like *The New Invisible Man* (1958), *Billy the Kid versus Dracula* (1966), *Blackenstein* (1973) and *Legend of the Werewolf* (1974). Softcover (394 pp/5.5" X 8.5") Suggested Retail: $17.95

Written at an intermediate reading level for the kid in all of us, these picture books will take you back to your youth. In the spirit of the old Ian Thorne books are covered *Nabonga* (1944), *White Pongo* (1945) and more! Hardcover/Softcover (44 pp/7.5" X 9.25") Suggested Retail: $17.95(hc)/$9.99(sc) ISBN: 978- 1-7341546-9-6 (hc) 978- 1-7344730-5-6 (sc)

Written at an intermediate reading level for the kid in all of us, these picture books will take you back to your youth. In the spirit of the old Ian Thorne books are covered *The Lost World* (1925), *The Land That Time Forgot* (1975) and more! Hardcover/Softcover (44 pp/7.5" X 9.25") Suggested Retail: $17.95 (hc)/$9.99(sc) ISBN: 978-1-7344730 -6-3 (hc) 978- 1-7344730-7-0 (sc)

Written at an intermediate reading level for the kid in all of us, these picture books will take you back to your youth. In the spirit of the old Ian Thorne books are covered *Them!* (1954), *Empire of the Ants* (1977) and more! Hardcover/ Softcover (44 pp/7.5" X 9.25") Suggested Retail: $17.95(hc)/ $9.99(sc) ISBN: 978-1-7347816 -3-2 (hc) 978 -1-7347816-2-5 (sc)

THE BICEP BOOKS CATALOGUE

CRYPTOZOOLOGY/COWBOYS & SAURIANS

Cowboys & Saurians: Prehistoric Beasts as Seen by the Pioneers explores dinosaur sightings from the pioneer period via real newspaper reports from the time. Well-known cases like the Tombstone Thunderbird are covered along with more obscure cases like the Crosswicks Monster and more. Softcover (357 pp/5.06" X 7.8") Suggested Retail: $19.95 ISBN: 978-1-7341546-1-0

Cowboys & Saurians: Ice Age zeroes in on snowbound saurians like the Ceratosaurus of the Arctic Circle and a Tyrannosaurus of the Tundra, as well as sightings of Ice Age megafauna like mammoths, glyptodonts, Sarkastodons and Sabertoothed tigers. Tales of a land that time forgot in the Arctic are also covered. Softcover (264 pp/5.06" X 7.8") Suggested Retail: $14.99 ISBN: 978-1-7341546-7-2

Southerners & Saurians takes the series formula of exploring newspaper accounts of monsters in the pioneer period with an eye to the Old South. In addition to dinosaurs are covered Lizardmen, Frogmen, giant leeches and mosquitoes, and the Dingocroc, which might be an alien rather than a prehistoric survivor. Softcover (202 pp/5.06" X 7.8") Suggested Retail: $13.99 ISBN: 978-1-7344730-4-9

Cowboys & Saurians South of the Border explores the saurians of Central and South America, like the Patagonian Plesiosaurus that was really an lemisch, plus tales of the Neo-Mylodon, a menacing monster from underground called the Minhocao, Glyptodonts, and even Bolivia's three-headed dinosaur! Softcover (412 pp/ 5.06"X7.8") Suggested Retail: $17.95 ISBN: 978-1-953221-73-5

UFOLOGY/THE REAL COWBOYS & ALIENS IN CONJUNCTION WITH ROSWELL BOOKS

The Real Cowboys and Aliens: Early American UFOs explores UFO sightings in the USA between the years 1800-1864. Stories of encounters sometimes involved famous figures in U.S. history such as Lewis and Clark, and Thomas Jefferson.Hardcover (242pp/6" X 9") Softcover (262 pp/5.06" X 7.8") Suggested Retail: $24.99 (hc)/$15.95(sc) ISBN: 978-1-7341546-8-9\(hc)/978-1-7344730-8-7(sc)

The second entry in the series, *Old West UFOs*, covers reports spanning the years 1865-1895. Includes tales of Men in Black, Reptilians, Spring-Heeled Jack, Sasquatch from space, and other alien beings, in addition to the UFOs and airships. Hardcover (276 pp/6" X 9") Softcover (308 pp/5.06" X 7.8") Suggested Retail: $29.95 (hc)/$17.95(sc) ISBN: 978-1-7344730-0-1 (hc)/ 978-1-73447 30-2-5 (sc)

The third entry in the series, *The Coming of the Airships*, encompasses a short time frame with an incredibly high concentration of airship sightings between 1896-1899. The famous Aurora, Texas, UFO crash of 1897 is covered in depth along with many others. Hardcover (196 pp/6" X 9") Softcover (222 pp/5.06" X 7.8") Suggested Retail: $24.99 (hc)/$15.95(sc) ISBN: 978-1-7347816 -1-8 (hc)/978-1-7347816-0-1(sc)

Early 20th Century UFOs kicks off a new series that investigates UFO sightings of the early 1900s. Includes tales of UFOs sighted over the *Titanic* as it sunk, Nikola Tesla receiving messages from the stars, an alien being found encased in ice, and a possible virus from outer space.Hardcover (196 pp/6" X 9") Softcover (222 pp/5.06" X 7.8") Suggested Retail: $27.99 (hc)/$16.95(sc) ISBN: 978-1-7347816-1-8 (hc)/978-1-7347816-0-1(sc)

LOST FILMS FANZINE BACK ISSUES

THE LOST FILMS FANZINE VOL.1

ISSUE #1 SPRING 2020 The lost Italian cut of *Legend of Dinosaurs and Monster Birds* called *Terremoto 10 Grado*, plus *Bride of Dr. Phibes* script, *Good Luck! Godzilla*, the King Kong remake that became a car commercial, Bollywood's lost *Jaws* rip-off, Top Ten Best Fan Made Godzilla trailers plus an interview with Scott David Lister. 60 pages. Three variant covers/editions (premium color/basic color/b&w)

ISSUE #2 SUMMER 2020 How 1935's *The Capture of Tarzan* became 1936's *Tarzan Escapes*, the Orca sequels that weren't, Baragon in Bollywood's *One Million B.C.*, unmade *Kolchak: The Night Stalker* movies, *The Norliss Tapes*, *Superman V: The New Movie*, why there were no *Curse of the Pink Panther* sequels, *Moonlight Mask: The Movie*. 64 pages. Two covers/editions (basic color/b&w)

ISSUE #3 FALL 2020 *Blob* sequels both forgotten and unproduced, *Horror of Dracula* uncut, *Franken-stein Meets the Wolfman* and talks, myths of the lost *King Kong* Spider-Pit sequence debunked, the *Carnosaur* novel vs. the movies, *Terror in the Streets* 50th anniversary, *Bride of Godzilla* 55th Unniversary, Lee Powers sketchbook. 100 pages. Two covers/editions (basic color/b&w)

ISSUE #4 WINTER 2020/21 *Diamonds Are Forever's* first draft with Goldfinger, *Disciple of Dracula* into *Brides of Dracula*, *War of the Worlds* That Weren't Part II, *Day the Earth Stood Still II* by Ray Bradbury, *Deathwish 6*, *Atomic War Bride*, *What Am I Doing in the Middle of a Revolution?*, *Spring Dream in the Old Capital* and more. 70 pages. Two covers/editions (basic color/b&w)

THE LOST FILMS FANZINE VOL.2

ISSUE #5 SPRING 2021 The lost films and projects of ape suit performer Charles Gemora, plus *Superman Reborn*, *Teenage Mutant Ninja Turtles IV: The Next Mutation*, *Mikado Zombie*, NBC's *Big Stuffed Dog*, King Ghidorah flies solo, *Grizzly II* reviewed, and War of the Worlds That Weren't concludes with a musical. Plus Blu-Ray reviews, news, and letters. 66 pages. Two covers/editions (basic color/ b&w)

ISSUE #6 SUMMER 2021 Peter Sellers *Romance of the Pink Panther*, Akira Kurosawa's *Song of the Horse*, *Kali - Devil Bride of Dracula*, Jack Black as Green Lantern, *Ladybug, Ladybug*, lost superhero Hiyo Man, and *Lord of Light*, the CIA's covert movie that inspired 2012's *Argo*. Plus news, Blu-Ray reviews, and letters. 72 pages. Two covers/editions (basic color/b&w)

ISSUE #7 FALL 2021 *Hiero's Journey*, Don Bragg in *Tarzan and the Jewels of Opar*, DC's *Lobo* movie, Lee Powers Scrapbook returns, Blake Matthews uncovers *The Big Boss Part II* (1976), Matthew B. Lamont searches for lost Three Stooges, and an ape called Kong in 1927's *Isle of Sunken Gold*. Plus news, and letters. 72 pages. Two covers/editions (basic color /b&w)

ISSUE #8 WINTER 2021/22 The connection between Steve Reeves' unmade third Hercules movie and *Goliath and the Dragon*, *The Iron Man* starring Tom Cruise, Phil Yordan's *King Kong* remake, *The Unearthly Stranger*, *Saturday Super-cade* forgotten cartoon, the 45th anniversary of Luigi Cozzi's "Cozzilla" and *Day the Earth Froze*. Plus news and letters. 72 pages. Two covers/editions (basic color /b&w)

MOVIE MILESTONES BACK ISSUES

MOVIE MILESTONES VOL. 1 — VOL. 2

ISSUE #1 AUGUST 2020 Debut issue celebrating 80 years of *One Million B.C.* (1940), and an early 55th Anniversary for *One Million Years B.C.* (1966). Abandoned ideas, casting changes, and deleted scenes are covered, plus, a mini-B.C. stock-footage filmography and much more! 54 pages. Three collectible covers/editions (premium color/basic color/b&w)

ISSUE #2 OCTOBER 2020 Celebrates the joint 50th Anniversaries of *When Dinosaurs Ruled the Earth* (1970) and *Creatures the World Forgot* (1971). Also includes coverage at *Prehistoric Women* (1967), *When Women Had Tails* (1970), and *Caveman* (1981), plus unmade films like *When the World Cracked Open*. 72 pages. Three collectible covers/editions (premium color/basic color/b&w)

ISSUE #3 WINTER 2021 Japanese 'Panic Movies' like *The Last War* (1961), *Submersion of Japan* (1973), and *Bullet Train* (1975) are covered on celebrated author Sakyo Komatsu's 90th birthday. The famous banned Toho film *Prophecies of Nostradamus* (1974) are also covered. 124 pages. Three collectible covers/editions (premium color/basic color/b&w)

ISSUE #4 SPRING 2021 This issue celebrates the joint 60th Anniversaries of *Gorgo, Reptilicus* and *Konga* examining unmade sequels like *Reptilicus 2*, and other related lost projects like *Kuru Island* and *The Volcano Monsters*. Also explores the Gorgo, Konga and Reptilicus comic books from Charlton. 72 pages. Three collectible covers/editions (premium color/basic color/b&w)

MOVIE MILESTONES VOL. 2 — VOL. 3 COMING SOON

ISSUE #5 SUMMER 2021 *Godzilla vs. the Sea Monster* gets the spotlight, with an emphasis on its original version *King Kong vs. Ebirah*, plus information on *The King Kong Show* which inspired it, and Jun Fukuda's tangentially related ed spy series *100 Shot/100 Killed*. 72 pages. Three collectible covers/editions (premium color /basic color/b&w)

ISSUE #6 FALL 2021 Monster Westerns of the 1950s and 1960s are spotlighted in the form of *Teenage Monster, The Curse of the Undead, Billy the Kid Versus Dracula, Jesse James Meets Frankenstein's Daughter*, and Bela Lugosi's unmade *The Ghoul Goes West*. 50 pages. Special Black and White exclusive!

ISSUE #7 WINTER 2022 This issue is all about Amicus's Edgar Rice Burroughs trilogy including *Land That Time Forgot, At the Earth's Core, People That Time Forgot* plus unmade sequels like *Out of Time's Abyss* or Doug McClure as John Carter of Mars. All this plus *Warlords of Atlantis* and *Arabian Adventure!* 100 pages. Three collectible covers/editions (premium color /basic color/b&w)

ISSUE #8 SPRING 2022 *Godzilla vs. Gigan* turns 50 and this issue is here to celebrate with its many unmade versions, like *Godzilla vs. the Space Monsters* and *Return of King Ghidorah*, plus *The Mysterians* 65th anniversary and *Daigoro vs. Goliath's* 50th.

Twenty-six years ago, outlaw Billy the Kid's tombstone was stolen from Fort Sumner, New Mexico. Now it has mysteriously been returned. When teenage brothers Pancho and Dorado Dumez steal it themselves, they get more than they bargained for. Encased inside the tombstone is a map that leads to the Southwest's greatest treasure: The Lost Adams Diggings—a canyon comprised of solid gold. But the brothers aren't the only ones on the treasure's trail. So is bounty hunter Seven McCaw, and along with him comes a modern-day incarnation of the Santa Fe Ring—a secretive organization that once ruled the West. Forced onto the open roads of New Mexico, the brothers must solve the mystery of Billy the Kid's death and find the lost canyon before the Ring does...

Printed in Great Britain
by Amazon